GOD WON

*How twelve steps
revealed the Good News
of the Gospel*

Donald C. Wes

ISBN 978-1-64416-034-3 (paperback)
ISBN 978-1-64458-251-0 (hardcover)
ISBN 978-1-64416-035-0 (digital)

Christian Faith Publishing, Inc.
832 Park Avenue
Meadville, PA 16335
www.christianfaithpublishing.com

Printed in the United States of America

CONTENTS

ACKNOWLEDGMENT

I would be remiss without first giving many thanks and gratitude to the AA fellowship in general, my AA sponsor Walt, all my AA family, many good friends in my various AA home groups, and all my brothers in Christ in my Bible Study Fellowship groups over the years. I also give acknowledgment to all those who encourage me to write this book, including my wife Cheryl, senior pastor Steve Williams, of Grace Community Church in Seal Beach CA along with the Rt. Reverend Patrick Bell, Bishop of the Eastern Oregon Diocese of the Episcopal Church.

I further give acknowledgment and heartfelt thanks for my loving and supportive family. All of my adult children (often without knowing) have played a very large part in my recovery. To my three sons, Trent, Chris, and Edsel, I express a deep and sincere gratitude for our everlasting bond of true love and honest friendship.

To my beautiful, loving, and supportive daughters, Amy and Kendall, who I treasure both so deeply. Amy was so precious when we first met; at five years old, she wanted her mom to marry me from the very beginning. Amy has always known what she wants in life and goes and gets it. And sure enough, Amy's mom took her advice at five years old and eventually married me.

And of course, my miracle baby, Kendall, has meant everything to me. My deep and boundless love for my daughter, Kendall was a primary source behind my need to change my ways. Not only has Kendall's true love been instrumental in my new transformed life, but she has also been the glue that has brought our whole family together.

Last but not least, I would not be here today without my dear, loving wife. There are not enough adjectives to describe what Cheryl means to me. She is the most loving, patient, caring, selfless, and Christ-devoted person that I have ever known. She stood by me through all my trials with love and support. She never wavered. Even when she realized that there was little she could do, she encouraged me to seek help and most important, she always prayed for me. Her prayers worked as God used her to save my life. Thank you to my family and thank you God for these blessings.

Finally, I give all the glory to God!

PREFACE

I n this book, I offer my story about a long and merciless struggle with alcoholism to illustrate the human tragedy that we all encounter with a life that is void of the presence of God. In fact, the crux of the story is not about alcoholism, but an ongoing battle with God. In this book, I begin by chronicling a tragic story of a life driven by self-centered fear that was caused by pride. In general, this prideful problem of self-centeredness is a familiar predicament to all humankind in varying degrees. To alleviate our plight, an enormous price has to be paid.

My story is similar to what many people experience who struggle with addictions or for that matter any sinful way of life that separates them from God. I lived a life in constant rebellion against God, but at the same time professed a belief in God. I was ambitious and well accomplished in both my professional life and family life, but rarely felt satisfied or having any sense of contentment. I was blind to most of my problems and incapable of being honest with myself. In fact, I viewed alcohol as the solution to my problems. For others, their answer might be found in anything from prescription drug abuse to an obsession with shopping or addiction to their work. For me, it was the drink that provided the comfort that I was seeking to cover up my perceived inadequacies. It was all about building a façade that looked good on the outside. On the inside, I was embroiled in an on-going battle with God. I lived in constant fear that my deficiencies may be uncovered. In the last days of my disease, my life was a living hell, and I was running scared.

My story is not about alcoholism. In fact, addiction was not the core problem; it was a symptom. The cause of my troubles was self-centered fear or if you will, pride. This prideful problem is a familiar story. Many of us live it. Pride is the sin of looking to our "self" as our god. The bigger dilemma was my inability to see my false pride as a problem. In fact, I regarded my pride and self-sufficiency as a virtue. Near the end, it was my refusal to recognize the truth that made a very severe illness, nearly fatal.

In this book, I use my story as a real-life illustration to establish a proven pathway out of the predicament that we all encounter. I found the solution in two significant books: (1) The Bible and (2) Alcoholics Anonymous (Big Book). The Big Book was derived from the Bible, and I found no contradictions between the two. The New Testament of the Bible gives us the good news of the Gospel where God has provided us the "Way, the Truth and the Life" (John 14:6) through His Son Jesus Christ, which is our only hope. The Twelve Steps of the Big Book takes us step by step to a spiritual awakening and the promise that only God can restore us to sobriety and a new life of recovery. This book is not about my explanation of how it works, but that it does work—it really does. There may not be an adequate explanation, but there is a formulation that works.

The overriding message that I make in this book is that the solution is not an intellectual exercise, but an action plan. The action steps may seem simple, but the application is not easy. In fact, applying these principles is the hardest thing I have ever done. As Bill W. says in the Big Book, "Simple, but not easy; a price had to be paid. It meant the destruction of self-centeredness."

I describe in this book the power of the fellowship of Alcoholics Anonymous (AA) and by working the action plan of the Twelve Steps resulted in a life-saving spiritual awakening. But more importantly, I demonstrate through my story how a spiritual awakening and the promises of the Twelve Steps revealed the good news of the Gospel. And the Gospel of Jesus Christ not only saved my life but gave me a whole new life.

My purpose in writing this book is first and foremost to glorify God. It is by His loving grace that my life was saved, but more importantly, I was given this new God-centered life. By His grace, I have become a bondservant to Christ Jesus. I have no means of paying back this debt, but God has commanded me to carry the message and to encourage those who are lost and still suffer. In the writing of this book, I do not presume to teach or preach in any way. This book represents my witness of God's message in my flesh. God has liberated me thus allowing my testimony the potential to inspire others. Hence, the writing of this book is my humble attempt to give away what was so freely given to me. If nothing else, the writing of this book has continued to help me grow in Christ as well as improve my relationships with my fellows.

The audience for this book includes anyone who is lost and broken due to alcohol addiction or suffers from any other sinful obsession. Hopefully, the allure of this book would extend to all who are searching for greater meaning in their life. In this book, I provide a practical action plan to achieve a transformed life by combining the twelve-step program with the Gospel of Jesus Christ. I do not present an intellectual exercise, but an action plan that works. Secondly, it is my hope that this book will encourage the clergy and other professional councilors to better understand the twelve-step program as a faith-based agenda that incorporates Christian values and is a valuable resource that should not be ignored. Thirdly, this book is designed to help Christian alcoholics to realize that even with God in their lives; an alcoholic needs the AA fellowship to stay sober. Finally, the AA program, like the Gospel, is a lifelong endeavor that must be practiced on a daily basis. There is no final destination for us to reach in this lifetime.

As the Big Book explains, "We are not cured of alcoholism. What we really have is a daily reprieve contingent on the maintenance of our spiritual conditions." More importantly, it doesn't matter if we are a leper, alcoholic, liar, thief, cheat, or just a garden-variety sinner; our loving God has provided all of us a way out. Glory be to God!

Author's Notes

The reader of this book may take notice that there is some redundancy in the book. However, there is a credible rationale in repeating certain trustworthy principles. The purpose of reiterating these ideas is the belief that absolute truths must be fully embraced as we progress further. "My Story" put forth a pathway to the truth which incorporates a few powerful ideas that I feel must be fully mastered to find peace with God. With this in mind, the following points are noteworthy in our quest for the truth: (1) we are all sinners and at war with God, (2) pain is the price of admission to the new life, (3) God paid the price with His love, (4) we all have a great decision to make that is the key to our lives, (5) we can't fix ourselves—our only hope is with Christ Jesus, (6) it takes a spiritual awakening and not an intellectual persuasive argument to reveal the Good News of the Gospel, and finally (7) we can't serve two masters—Godley men glorify God and not self.

1. Our War with God—we are all Sinners.

Most of us do not believe that we are at war with God. We may believe that we are sinners, but most of us also feel that we are not that bad. In fact, the idea that we are *not that bad* creates our greatest stumbling-block to reconciliation with God. Hence, it is of paramount importance that we come to grips with the basic truth of the depravity of humankind. The book of Genesis describes how Adam and Eve turned away from God and decided that they could do better on their own without God. The Bible chronicles from the beginning how humankind inherited its self-centered prideful ways as described in the book of Genesis. Adam and Eve's contagion spread spiritual death through sin and, therefore, we all live in a fallen world in need of a savior.

Apostle Paul is vehement in describing the sinful nature of all humankind in Romans 3: 10-12— *"There is no one righteous, not even one; there is no one who understands; there is no one who seeks God. All have turned away, they have together become worthless; there is no one who does good, not even one."* Paul is so insistent that all of humankind is at odds with God that he repeats himself *("there is no one…")* several times in these verses. The Bible describes the depravity of man as the definitive problem that we all face. In fact, if we are unable to understand that humankind is born with a spiritual depravity, we cannot understand ourselves, our fellows, or the world we live in. Therefore, self-centered pride is our conundrum and we must clearly define this problem before we can find a way out.

The Big Book defines the problem of alcoholism as a spiritual malady. A malady is defined as a disease, disorder, or an unwholesome condition. The Big Book says, *"First of all, we had to quit playing God. It didn't work."* The Big Book defines the problem further by saying, *"Selfishness—self-centeredness! That we think, is the root of our troubles. Driven by a hundred forms of fear, self-delusion, self-seeking and self-pity…They arise out of ourselves, and the alcoholic is an extreme example of self-will run riot."* The heart of the problem is that the focus of the nature of man is all about himself or if you like—pride.

Before any solution can be developed, a clear definition of the problem must be identified. Hence, the importance of not just understanding, but emphatically embracing the absolute truth that we all start out as rebels against God.

2. Pain is the Price of Admission to a New Life.

The Twelve-Step program suggests that trials and tribulations are touchstones to spiritual growth. However, our natural instincts are to run away from pain and suffering by seeking comfort. But comfort is not something that we should seek. As C. S. Lewis says, *"If we seek comfort, we will never find the truth; but if we seek the truth, we will receive comfort along the way."* The Twelve-Step program claims that pain and hardship is the pathway to truth. In fact, the twelve-by-twelve states, *"In every case, pain had been the price of admission into a new life. But this admission price had purchased more than we expected. It brought a measure of humility, which we soon discover to be a healer of pain."* This becomes our turning point when we begin to see humility as the solution to our problem of pride. The twelve-by-twelve goes on to say, *"Many of us who had thought ourselves religious awoke to the limitations of this attitude. Refusing to place God first, we had deprived ourselves of His help. But now the words 'Of myself I am nothing, the Father doeth the works' began to carry bright promise and meaning."* Hence, the significant turning point in our lives comes when we finally humble ourselves to God.

Humility is the solution and we began to realize that humility is the spiritual foundation for both the Gospel and the Twelve-Step Recovery program. This is where we give up all pretenses and accept our proper place in our relationship to God and our fellows.

Scripture describes throughout the Bible how humility is the foundation of our salvation. The Bible says in James 4:4-7, *"So humble yourself before God. Resist the devil, and he will flee from you. Come close to God, and God will come close to you."* As Jesus said in the Sermon on the Mount, *"Blessed are the poor in spirit, for theirs is the kingdom of heaven. Blessed are those who mourn…Blessed are the meek, for they will inherit the earth"* (Matthew 5: 3-5). In other words, we cannot experience God-blessed salvation without true humility. As Jesus described in the parable of the Pharisee and Tax Collector, the boastful Pharisee did not find favor before God, but the tax collector admitted his faults and humbly asked for mercy for his sinful ways. Jesus said, *"I tell you this sinner, not the Pharisee, returned home justified before God. For those who exalt themselves will be humbled, and those who humble themselves will be exalted"* (Luke 18:14). Jesus makes the point clear that we cannot earn our way to salvation. But by coming clean with an honest assessment of our wrongdoings and humbly asking for mercy, we will be justified before God. It is the humble of heart and not the boastful that receive God's favor.

3. God paid the Price with His Love.

The Big Book talks about the simplicity of the program but also recognizes that it is not easy. This may be an understatement. Bill W. says in his story, *"Simple but not easy; a price had to be paid. It meant the destruction of self-centeredness."* Bill went on to say, *"I must turn in all things to the Father of Light who presides over us all."* This destruction of self-centeredness is tantamount to coming to the Cross of Christ crucified. Out of a state of desperation, we strip our pride and humble ourselves to our God at the foot of the Cross.

God accomplished the greatest event in human history. God gave us His love through His Son on the Cross. A price has to be paid. And God paid that price through His Son on the Cross. The Cross of Christ is the gate by which all humankind can enter into oneness with God. He is *"the Lamb who was slain from the foundation of the world"* (Revelation 13:8). God came in the flesh to take away our sins and nothing else. The Cross is where the holiness of God collides with the sinfulness of man. But it is not the sinful man that bears the cost and pain of this collision; It is God's love that pays the price.

4. The Great Decision—the Key to your Life.

God's plan of salvation was put into place at the foundation of the world. The Father has planned for our salvation. The Son has purchased our salvation on the cross and the Holy Spirit applies our salvation to our daily lives. God has done His part; it is now time for us to do our part. We need only to make a choice with our free will.

The Third step from the Big Book says, *"Made a decision to turn our will and our lives over to the care of God as we understand Him."* The program asks us to muster up the willingness to make a decision to allow our will to conform to the will of God. The effectiveness of the whole program rests on how well and earnestly we have come to this decision.

Our part is to make the decision of a lifetime. The Bible says that this is a choice between life and death. God spoke through Moses in Deuteronomy 30:15–20, *"Now listen! Today I am giving you a choice between life and death; between prosperity and disaster . . . You can make this choice by loving the Lord your God, obeying Him, and committing yourself firmly to Him. This is the key to your life."*

We are at a fork in the road. The choice is binary—we either stay on our current self-centered path or we choose the God-centered path that has been laid out in front of us. This is the most difficult and important decision of our life. It is a matter of herculean courage to make the ultimate decision to surrender to the process. The Big Book says, *"...crushed by a self-imposed crisis we could not postpone or evade, we had to fearlessly face the proposition that God is everything or else He is nothing. God either is or He isn't. What is your choice to be?"* Choose to live or choose a spiritual death. The great spiritual paradox is that victory is won by surrender.

5. We can't fix Ourselves—Our only hope is with Christ Jesus.

Hope does not come naturally to most of us. In fact, to find hope, our only chance is to look to God. The Big Book gives us hope by stating, *"That no human power could have relieved our alcoholism...but God could and would if He were sought."* It is only through trusting in God that we are able to step out of the darkness into the light and begin to feel the rays of hope. As C. S. Lewis says, *"Believing in Christianity is like believing in the rising sun, it's not simply that you can see it, but by it you can see everything else."* The Bible explains that the death of Christ was the darkest hour for His disciples. But with the resurrection, that despair turned to hope. In John 14: 6 God provides us the *"way and the truth and the life. No one comes to the Father except through me."* In the Bible, hope is a firm conviction through prophesy that the future promises of God will be fulfilled. Both the Old and New Testament point to our only hope is through His son Jesus Christ.

6. Spiritual Awakening vs. Intellectual Argument.

The miracle of the AA program rests solidly on the foundation of this gift of a new life through a spiritual awakening as the result of working the twelve steps. Both the Bible and the Big Book disavowal any notion that the pathway to truth is gained by an intellectual exercise. In the Bible, Jesus says that we must receive the kingdom of God like a little child. The Big Book maintains that a spiritual awakening will come about as a result of practicing action steps vs. an intellectual argument.

The Bible speaks about the spiritual blindness that renders us incapable of grasping our need for God's help. Without this recognition and the guidance of God through His spirit, we will not comprehend the Bible. We may think that we grasp the Word, but it will remain veiled. Apostle Paul says in 1 Corinthian 2:14, *"The man without the Spirit does not accept the things that come from the Spirit of God, for they are foolishness to him, and he cannot understand them because they are spiritually discerned."*

The Big Book describes the beginning of the spiritual awakening in step 3 as follows: *"as we become conscious of His presence, we begin to lose our fear of today, tomorrow or the hereafter. We were reborn."* The Bible says that we must be "born again" to enter the kingdom of God. Jesus replied, *"Very truly I tell you, no one can see the kingdom of God unless they are born again"* (John 3:3). In both cases, we receive a new life, a spiritual life through the spirit of God in us. Without the spirit of God in us, we remain lost and unable to find our way.

7. We can't serve two Masters—Godly Men glorify God not self.

The greatest evidence of my new life in Christ is that I no longer feel the need to prove myself. Today I have but one master—almighty God. Before, I had many masters. I hid behind my mask and cared only about my outward appearance in an effort please everyone. Even though I would not admit it, I had all the idols of wealth, fame and/or prestige, and a whole lot of pride. The AA program suggests that *what other people think about us is none of our business.'* Today, with my only master being my God, there is little fear, worry or need to prove myself. I have given up all pretenses. I no longer need to hide behind my façade, which created so many of my fears.

Godly men glorify God, but Godless men glorify self. Scripture talks about how we cannot serve two masters. The Bible says, *"I care little if I am judged by you or by any human court; indeed, I do not even judge myself"* (1 Corinthians 4:3). God is my owner by creation and also my owner by right of purchase. I was bought at a price--the precious blood of Jesus Christ.

CHAPTER I

My Story

ACT I-OLD MAN

1. It Wasn't Supposed to End Like This

It was just another trial preparation meeting with my team of trial lawyers sitting in a glass-enclosed high-rise conference room in downtown LA overlooking the famous Hollywood sign in the nearby hillsides below. These meetings had become a commonplace experience for me since I had been the center of several corporate trials and investigations before this. Being the center of focus of this meeting with several lawyers, clerks, piles of paper, briefs, laptops, a stream of numbered documents and exhibits being shuffled around the table and pushed in front of me for comment, was becoming tiresome. For the most part, I had become the primary expert on the case since I was targeted as "the most knowledgeable person" in several lawsuits that had named me personally as a vital officer of the corporation. The corporation itself was also named along with every member of the board of directors.

This particular meeting, however, carried more weight than others because time was running out on our final preparations for a fast approaching trial date. The discovery process had gone on for the better part of two years. I had been engaged in countless meetings of defending myself and educating various lawyers, consultants, investigators, as well as some of my associates regarding our cutting-edge business strategies. I firmly believed that our strategic vision was always within reasonable "safe harbors" of legal activity. The feelings that I was encountering on this day may have been much like the preparation for any major event, which entailed years of practice. Much like that of a championship sports team in their final practice sessions before the big game after a season of training camp practices, scrimmages, regular season games, playoff eliminations, and now the final preparation for the game of their lives—"the championship." Each player must be fully prepared to stay cool under pressure.

This trial was my "big game." The stress had been building, but I had been trained all my life to stay cool under pressure. Never show fear and keep calm at all costs. As a leader, we are not allowed to show weakness. We were expected to exhibit strength, but what my legal team did not know, and even I was not fully aware of at the time, was a problem of catastrophic proportions that was brewing inside of me. The legal team was fully aware of the problem of my poor performance during previous depositions. We were now preparing for my courtroom testimony and how to walk back several miss statements that I had made during depositions taken under oath.

As I sat in this meeting with my stomach churning and that warm sweat beginning to bead up upon my forehead, I was becoming overwhelmed with anxiety and fear. It was like a panic attack brewing inside me like something that I had never experienced before. I felt trapped with no way out. I was overwhelmed with fear and knew that someway and somehow I had to come clean.

I turned to Dave, my lead counsel and the partner in charge of this case, and asked for a short restroom break. As I left the room, I said quietly to Dave, "We need to chat privately upon my return. I think it is important that we talk."

Upon my return, the conference room was empty except for Dave standing in the corner with a glass of ice water gazing out at the view of the Hollywood sign in the distance below as if he was waiting for some bombshell to hit. I proceeded to pour myself a glass of ice water and suggested that we both have a seat. I took a deep breath and paused to collect my thoughts and said, "Dave . . . I'm not prepared to go on trial. I'm not doing well."

His eyes opened wide, and his jaw dropped as I went on. "I'm hurting both physically, mentally, and emotionally."

With a measure of disgust, Dave responded in a way that strongly suggested that I had no choice. "This case is dependent on your testimony." Dave explained. "You are the key witness, and without your testimony, we have no case. This trial is not just about you, but the whole company and each member of the board of directors have a huge stake in a successful outcome." Dave carried on with increasing disgust, "Don, I don't know what has gotten into you. You can't just bail out on everyone days before trial after years of preparation." Dave continued in a very stern voice, "Don, you have no choice in the matter. We will carry on, and you will go on trial."

Finally, I responded by getting down and completely leveling with Dave like never before. For the first time, I was on the verge of exposing myself out of total desperation not only to Dave but myself, as well. I needed to get Dave's attention in a real way. My stomach was churning deep down with a sick feeling when I finally blurted, "Dave, I need help. I can't do it.

The stress of all these legal cases is taking a toll on me. I'm afraid my drinking is out of control. No longer can I cope without the drink. The problem has been building at an alarming pace which I can no longer keep under wraps. This drinking problem had been building slowly, but more recently, it has escalated to the point that I feel that suddenly I have fallen into a death spiral. The mounting stress has heightened my fears that lead to heavier drinking which cause more fear leading to more drink, and on and on. Dave," I said, "I'm going down fast. I am an alcoholic, and I need help."

Dave was simply stunned and was held speechless for a moment in which his disgust with me seemed to diminish a bit too some level of sympathy. In a more calm voice, Dave admitted, "In all my years of law practice and trying various cases, I have never encountered a situation like this. I'm at a loss. I'm not sure what to do or where we go from here."

As Dave carried on in search for a solution, my thoughts began to focus on my life and after all these years of the so-called "good life," questioning myself about, how did I get here? How did I arrive at this very dark place? It seemed as though I had reached a dead end. I felt trapped with no way out. The realization that I was indeed lost gave me a very sick feeling of total despair. In all my years of life, living with ups and downs, I had never felt such a sense of hopelessness. It wasn't supposed to end like this.

2. The Good Life

Being raised like many American boys, from a loving family of modest circumstances, attending public schools, in suburbia northwest of Los Angeles, I enjoyed my boyhood years with friends in school, playing sports, and being raised by a caring and loving family. I was the first of two sons of a young veteran of WWII. My father served as a naval officer in the Pacific during the war. My mother was an only child and suffered the loss of her mother at the young age of sixteen. Her mother suffered a traumatic and fatal brain hemorrhage collapsing to her death in my mother's arms. Her dying words to my mom were, "Always be a good girl."

My mother certainly lived up to her mom's dying request by being such a loving and caring mother to my younger brother and me. In fact, both of my parents were always there for me and very supportive. As an only child, until I was twelve years old, I was the center of the family, being the first child, grandchild, and also the first nephew to my only uncle (my dad's only brother) and aunt. For most of my boyhood, I was treated more adult-like than most kids my age, for I was usually the only child among adults at our family gatherings. Consequently, I was afforded more freedoms than most and seemed to acquire a bit more maturity for my age than many of my friends.

My childhood years, in the fifties consisted of growing up in middle-class suburbia. As a young boy, I loved sports and played Little League baseball. My first hero was Mickey Mantle until the Dodgers moved to LA and I became a lifelong Dodger fan with Don Drysdale and other Dodgers players becoming my new idols. My dad taught me how to play golf at twelve years old, and I watched Arnold Palmer winning Master golf tournaments on TV in the early sixties. About thirty years later, I had the privilege of playing golf with Arnold Palmer (the King) at his home course in Latrobe PA (I won a Skin from Palmer on the par five sixth hole with a Birdie to Palmer's Par). This was a lifetime experience and my only claim to fame in golf.

As the sixties rolled on, I spent summer days surfing at Malibu with some of the surfing world's icons of the day like Dewey Weber, Lance Carson, and Mickey Dora.

In my younger boyhood days, I enjoyed very wholesome family life. My mom and dad, however, were not religious; therefore I had no church upbringing. At about age eight, my mom asked me if I would be interested in attending church. On my own, I chose to participate in catechism class so we as a family could go to the Catholic Church. While my mom didn't have any religious upbringing or preference, my dad was raised in a Catholic community, although he was not a practicing Catholic. At an early age, I had a strong desire to know about God. I believe that I acquired this need to know God from my mother. Even though she had little or no religious upbringing, it was my mom who encouraged me to seek God. This may have been due to the tragic death of my mom's mom at such a young age. In any case, both my mom and I had a strong desire to know God. However, after my younger brother was born, we as a family quit going to church. Mom had her hands full raising both a newborn and a teenager. I didn't mind the attention shifting from me to my baby brother because as a growing teenager, I treasured some newfound freedom. Also, as I entered a more rebellious phase of life, the idea of organized religion began to fade. In looking back, it is interesting that my brother Craig who never experience church-life growing up has never developed or encouraged any faith in his life or his family's life.

I also had great ambition to succeed in life, which was instilled in me by my dad's strong work ethic. He owned a service station business and worked seven days a week until I was about seven years old. My parents were a very loving family. They had lots of friends and believed in hard work, and they played hard. The whole family was very social, and of course, drinking was always a centerpiece of their social activities.

My greatest love was playing sports throughout my school years. Even though I was the caption of the basketball team, I began working part-time in high school and continued working nonstop for the rest of my life even in retirement. With little savings from my part-time work, I was able to buy a car at sixteen and weekend party life became my primary focus for many years to come. I did well enough in high school to get by, while always looking to have a good time. Party-time weekend drinking was commonplace, and it helped me to be comfortable with being a part of the various social cliques in high school.

I graduated high school and began college in the mid-sixties. Drugs, alcohol, free love, and free spirit were prevalent on the college campus. I mostly stayed clear of the drug scene because it was illegal but enjoyed drinking, probably because it was so familiar to me from family gatherings, and it also provided me with much-needed social comfort. Instead of drugs, I took a keen interest in the eastern spiritualism trend, which was closely associated with the drug scene. I'm not sure why I liked spiritual teachings, except for the fact that I always had a strong desire to know God. Also, it was cool in the sixties to turn against organized religion and look to drugs, alcohol, and/ or mediation for our comfort pleasures. I tended to select alcohol and eastern meditation as my flavors of choice. Therefore, it was very natural for me to join a fraternity upon entering college in which drinking and party-time were the core values. Again, my ambition to succeed in life encourages me to stay in school and avoid the Vietnam War. College was not easy for me, but my drive to get ahead and fear of the draft kept my nose in the books allowing me to graduate with good enough grades to land a pretty good professional position right out of school.

Upon graduation, I not only landed a good job, but I also married my college sweetheart. We had gone together for most of our college years, and we were ready to begin a new promising life together. The dream had come true with everything falling into place. In time I became a financial officer of a major medical center, and we moved into a beautiful hillside neighborhood in hopes raising our family. But this wasn't enough. My drive for more success led me to open a pizzeria restaurant while keeping my professional position. This gave me the sense of being strong, aggressive, and independent. I was on my way to make my mark. I always admired my dad for being his own boss by owning his own business. Now I would not only measure up to my dad but even do better than him. I now had plenty to be proud of with a beautiful wife, great career, my own business and a lot of good friends.

3. Rocky Times Ahead

My drinking was just a regular part of my active social and business life. But success brought increased social and business activities and all my friends and associates drank on a regular basis. All activities became an occasion to drink whether it was an after-work gathering or the weekend of golf at the nineteenth hole. The cocktail hour became a daily routine. My wife also drank with me at home, so it didn't seem as noticeable when the quantities increased, and the occasions for a drink became more frequent.

Nearly eight years into our marriage, my wife and I began to realize that we may be unable to have children. After many trips to the doctor, it was determined that my wife's uterus problems were decreasing our chances of ever having a baby. This was not good news for either of us for we both had our heart set on having children and raising a family. My wife struggled more than me for she always wanted to be a mother in the worst way. This became a very unacceptable situation for her. It was now just a matter of time for this to develop into a major crisis in our lives.

I was oblivious to what was brewing in our marriage. Life was good with a beautiful marriage, successful, professional career, a growing business, and living in a beautiful hillside home in an upscale neighborhood. It couldn't get much better. So it was more than disturbing when my wife came home unusually late on Friday night, visibly shaken. She had no coherent excuse for this unusual behavior. So she finally came clean and explained that she had an affair and wanted a divorce. Just like that! This was unexpected, and I was utterly oblivious to any marital problems. My immediate reaction was that this was entirely unacceptable.

I told her divorce was out of the question. I explained to her that I had worked hard my whole life just to provide for her. She could not just walk out on me like that. If she had some problem with me, we could work it out. But I soon learned that I was not in control. She could and would do what she wanted, and there was nothing I could do about it.

This was just the first of another significant crisis to follow. But this one devastated me. Most of all, my pride was crushed. I felt like a failure. I also felt terrible shame. My wife gave me no good answer as to why she wanted out. She always kept most things to herself. But having no reasonable explanation when it comes to our marriage commitment seemed so unfair. I tried my best to examine what went wrong. Maybe it was not having a baby or possibly I was working too much and not paying enough attention to her. Of course, I didn't believe it was my drinking for she never complained about it. I never came to any solid conclusions, but as time passed, I did discover a couple of important lessons.

First, I'm not in control, and my life is unmanageable. No matter how hard I tried to fix things, it was not to be. I could not force it. And the sooner I was able to forgive and let go, the sooner life got better. For some reason and I do not know why I was able to let go. Indeed, life got better. Second, for the first time in my life, I discovered that my problem was due mostly to my self-centeredness. It became clear that the problem wasn't what I did, but what I didn't do. I was too preoccupied with myself to care for her needs. This is a difficult lesson for most of us to learn. Self-centeredness is a problem that will continue to haunt me throughout most of my life ahead.

Soon after my divorce, I suffered another major unexpected crisis. My dad's growing drinking problem had taken its toll on his ability to function at work. He was working for me at one of my pizzerias at the time. He had lost his service station business a few years prior due to the oil embargo in the early seventies. His drinking had escalated from the stresses of losing his business and livelihood. He was too young for retirement, so he invested some savings in my pizza restaurant and went to work for me. It was more than heartbreaking to ask my dad, my lifelong mentor, to leave his job and go home to my mom. My dad was the man I always admired. To me, he was a terrific dad which I had pattered my life after. I had no choice but to terminate him and organize an intervention to place him in an alcohol treatment program.

This was hard on me for I had such respect for my dad and had modeled much of my life after him. He did comply with the family wishes and entered the VA treatment program voluntarily. Unfortunately, he continued to struggle with sobriety after treatment for some time and to the point where I began to lose hope. He finally did get some long-term sobriety; however, he never embraced the AA program. Again, a couple of lessons were to be learned. First, alcohol is cunning, baffling, and powerful! And second, alcoholism does not discriminate. It doesn't matter if you are rich or poor, tall or short, or what your race or religion is. It is all powerful to an alcoholic. What I did not fully grasp at this time was that there is no controlling alcoholism. It always gets worse and never better and the harder you try to control it without help, the worse it gets.

The other overarching lesson to be learned is that life is always changing. I had thought that I had arrived. I had achieved the good life. This sense of contentment was suddenly shattered in a few short months. Life is never static; it will change, but then again, this too shall pass. In looking back, I see now that I entered a period of aimless searching. I was running scarred without any solid direction and nowhere to go. I was lost and all alone. My mom was able to provide me with some comfort, but I was too proud and self-sufficient to accept help from anyone.

4. Back in the Saddle

Even though I felt lost, it didn't take too long for me to get back in the saddle again. I soon developed an attitude that I had to prove myself again. I needed to show that I could pick myself up by my boot straps and get on with life. I began by putting all my energies into my work. With the help of a new partner, I developed a business expansion plan for my pizzeria restaurant to franchise into a regional chain operation. I also formed a consulting company with expertise in corporate strategic planning and business turnarounds in the healthcare industry.

Eventually, I became president and CEO for a client hospital corporation. I had achieved a successful turnaround and took charge of daily operations for a few years before ultimately selling the company to a syndicated investor group that I had sponsored.

My life was on the upswing again with new friends, business associates, and a few women who were taking an interest in me. My self-esteem had returned, and I began to become comfortable living on my own and achieving a reasonably successful professional career. The only thing missing was the family life. As much as I would like to get married again and raise a family, I was willing to accept whatever life had in store for me. Living in a coastal community, I took up sailing, cycling, and running for exercise. I felt like these activities could offset my growing drinking habit. I also took more interest in my other sports of snow skiing and golf. I had been divorced about four years and enjoying my life when one of the most exceptional events of my life happened.

I met and fell in love with my wife to be. She was and is perfect for me in almost every way. Cheryl was and is the most beautiful, loving, kind, considerate, and God-loving person I have ever met. Also, she had two beautiful children. Amy was just the cutest little five-year-old with blond hair and blue eyes, and Trent was a handsome brother four years older. This was like the perfect package where I get another chance to be a husband again and at the same time become a new father all at once.

Cheryl was recently divorced when we began dating. Her previous marriage was abusive, and it took its toll on her and the kids. I was sensitive to the situation and allowed the relationship to take its time. I didn't feel any need to rush it along. We both took it easy and let our relationship to grow naturally. This was very important for all four of us. The kids took to me reasonably well, especially Amy, and I discovered that I have a soft heart for cute little girls. I think that Trent took to me mostly because he liked my dog, a beautiful black lab named Arlo.

Arlo was my buddy and he soon became Trent's buddy as well. It was only a few months into our relationship when

Cheryl and I along with the kids were sitting in my living room at home. Amy came over to me while I was sitting in my chair. She leaned up against me, put her arm around me, and pressed her cheek to mine and said, "Mommy, can we marry him?" Wow! I don't remember how we responded to each other, but I do know that as awkward as it was, it felt good to me. At least Amy wanted to marry me. This certainly gave me a lift, but only time will tell. I enjoyed being a father figure to the kids, but again, I knew that I needed to take it easy.

Cheryl was the real parent. She was and is a great mother and now grandmother. Cheryl exhibited all the qualities of a great mom. She was loving, caring, and always there for her children. However, Cheryl kept firm with her rules. She stood by her principles and didn't back down. She was insistent on never making promises to the kids that she didn't follow through. Also, she never threatens them without being prepared to follow through if need be. Cheryl's parenting skills provided a great learning experience for me, and I took good note of it all.

The relationship continued to grow as we dated more often and we took the kids on family-type day trips to Catalina Island, Knots Berry Farm, and the like. As the CEO of my company, Cheryl would attend various work-related social functions with me. Even though I felt comfortable in my job, Cheryl at my side provided me with the much-needed security in my business social situations. She was the perfect complement to me and I felt that I complimented her as well. The relationship continued to grow as we begin to feel more and more comfortable with each other. Cheryl took a keen interest in my job. I worked hard at my job and even acted as though I enjoyed the stresses of being the top dog for my company. Even though Cheryl seemed to be proud of my position and was supporting in every way, I tried my best not to let it go to my head.

I admired Cheryl being a dedicated single working mom, attending college, and providing everything for her children. Her workload was unbelievable while at the same time she devoted any free time to paying attention to me. We grew together over time, making what would be a beautiful marriage and meld together a loving family. After four years of dating and falling desperately in love, we got married and built a new home in a beautiful neighborhood for the kids and us. I was a good provider for both her and the kids. We were and are deeply in love in an extraordinary relationship. This was indeed a gift from God.

I never thought twice about the idea that we would not be able to have a child together. Cheryl had explained long before we got married that she was unable to have any more children. Cheryl had her tubes tied after her last delivery. At that time, she chose to have her tubes tied so as not to have any more children in an unhappy marriage. What she did not count on was the divine intervention by God to receive a newly tested procedure of using rubber bands to tie the tubes rather than the standard method of cauterization. On that day about ten years prior, after Amy was born, Cheryl showed up late to be last in line to receive the outpatient procedure. After the two women before her had received the standard cauterization procedure, Cheryl was asked to give authorization to a new team of doctors to perform this experimental method of using bands vs. cauterization. Cheryl agreed, and the rest is history. These events have since proven was to be a miracle in the making in God's time.

Soon after our marriage, Cheryl had decided on her own that against all the odds she was going to have a reversal surgery on her tubes in the chance that she could get pregnant again with our child. I tried my best to explain, that even though I had always wanted to have my children, I was perfectly content being a stepfather to her children. We were both approaching our forties, and with her tubal surgery ten years prior, the likelihood of having a success seemed remote at best. However, she insisted on going through with it no matter what the odds. I conceded and began the search for the best GYN surgeon possible.

The surgery was not easy and took the precision of an experienced surgeon. Thank God that her tubes had not been cauterized ten years earlier. With the tubes tied with bands, there was a chance of success. The surgeon spoke to me the evening after the surgery explaining that it was a success. He went on to say that after sufficient recovery and a successful pregnancy, Cheryl could not have natural childbirth but would need to have a C-section instead. When I relayed this message to Cheryl the next morning, she was elated for her other two natural childbirths were not a pleasant experience. Sure enough, a few months after a long and complicated recovery from surgery, Cheryl was pregnant. This was another great event in our lives, against all the odds. Again, this is a miracle in the making.

The pregnancy went well. As the expectancy date got closer, we had the luxury to schedule a definite date for the C-section surgery. Everything was in place; all systems were on the go, the delivery date and time were scheduled. This time Cheryl and I showed up on time. Then on 7-11-88 (great numbers) at 9:00 a.m. in the morning, the miracle happened. Kendall Colleen was born. In the operating room, I cut the umbilical cord, and my baby girl was handed to me in my arms. Against all the odds, the miracle had happened, a gift from God. The next day, Trent and Amy could not wait to get to the hospital to see their new baby sister. A new family had been born, and our beautiful baby Kendall was the center that would bond us all together. Life had become a continual blessing.

Kendall was such a beautiful baby and had such an easy disposition. This proved to be the case all through her childhood. Family life could not be much better. Cheryl was the matriarch, and I played the role as head of the house and the primary provider. Because of Cheryl's experience, we became an excellent parenting partnership. As much as the kids tried to separate us, we were able to stay on the same page consistently. With our new baby girl, a beautiful loving marriage was growing ever so much stronger. This had developed into an extraordinary loving relationship more than I had ever dreamed.

5. Living the Dream

As a new family starting out, we had many advantages. First of all, we had more than a stable financial situation given my professional and business success. Secondly, Cheryl provided a mature firm parenting culture. Finally, and most important, Cheryl brought a robust Christian belief structure to our family. All the kids attended a private Christian school, and we became a strong churchgoing family. This was all relatively new to me, but I fully embraced it all. It felt so terrific and wholesome. Again, Cheryl was the matriarch and I was the provider.

It wasn't long after Kendall's birth that I sold the hospital company that I had turned around to an investor group. My business partner and I were also in the process of selling off our pizzeria restaurant chain, which had encountered tough economic times. Now that I was a family man with real responsibilities, I thought it would be best to consolidate my business life into a less stressful and more secure employment situation. My attitude was changing toward a less risky and more stable work life to devote more time to family responsibilities. Fortunately, I had garnered a wealth of strategic business experience, which served me well with several senior executive employment opportunities.

I took a senior executive position with an expanding hospital corporation. Reporting to both the CEO and the board, I was asked to develop new innovative corporate structures that would enable both nonprofit and for-profit corporations to merge to better position the company in a growing competitive healthcare marketplace. This entailed educating both management and the board to think outside of the box. It would also have a dramatic impact on the medical staff of the hospital as well as the community at large. Hospital corporations are incredibly complicated, very political with many vital stakeholders. I found this to be a fascinating challenge that would lead the way to revolutionize the delivery of healthcare in the community we served.

All change runs against fundamental human nature and makes most people uncomfortable. Even though I had a taste of the effect of change on the human condition by my previous experience in performing a hospital turnaround, I'm not sure I was fully prepared for the onslaught of negative attacks that I would need to endure in the coming years. I had no idea of the extent to which I would come under fire, but whatever the case, I was confident that I would be up for the challenge. In fact, I looked forward to it. I took tremendous pride in my capabilities in not only developing strategic vision but in my ability execute and successfully implement innovative change.

I loved my job. I always liked building new things. Developing new ways of approaching things was exciting to me. I was the architect. Even though I was a part of a team, I knew the "nuts and bolts" like nobody else. This knowledge gave me greater control than anybody else. I was required to be out in front and lead on many occasions, but I relished playing behind the scenes where I was most effectively in control. In effect, I could do it my way. Also, rarely could I be challenged because few knew the inner workings as I did. This need to be in control later proved to be vulnerability from which I could not run.

I knew how important it was to keep my family, social, and business life in proper balance. We could not afford for our marriage to fail especially in light of both Cheryl and my previous marriage failures and now with the responsibilities of the kids and our new baby daughter. My wife and family was now number one in my life with everything else taking second place. With this in mind, life became even more active. Fortunately, Cheryl was now able to become a stay-at-home mom for we had the financial means. Amy went to private Christian school while Trent went to a private military academy for stronger disciplinary needs.

Meanwhile, Kendall went to a private co-op preschool and daycare before entering Christian elementary school. While the kids were still young (before Trent entered high school), we took regular family vacations along with many family outings. As time went on, Trent and Amy spent more time with their friends and on occasion with their dad, leaving Cheryl and me more time with just Kendall. Since Kendall was eleven years younger than Amy, it was not long that she was being raised like an only child. We traveled a lot not only on vacations but also for my business reasons. All travel weather personal or business was pleasurable because both Cheryl and Kendall would be with me. Life was a pleasant blend of family, social, and professional activities. With such an active social life, it was only natural that drinking continued to be a growing part of daily life. It all seemed just to blend together and just as we must eat and sleep daily so did we work, play, and drink daily. My drinking habit was probably a bad influence on Cheryl for she seemed to enjoy our active, busy new life. However, as much as Cheryl did engage in social drinking she was always able to be more responsible with her alcohol. As much as she did enjoy it, she kept it well within proper bounds.

I always felt that we were nothing more than social drinkers. However, all our family members, friends, and workmates drank during most if not all social events. Whether it was a wedding, dinner party, golf outing, business conference, or any family gathering, drinking was always a central part of our activities. It all seemed so natural and I rarely if ever showed myself as drinking too much. I still maintained myself well in all social situations. In fact, I was always able to point to others who were unable to control their drinking. Even though my dad had crossed the line from being a social drinker to a problem alcoholic, neither Cheryl nor I had any concern about my drinking habit. Even in the social work environment, I was cautious to control my drinking. But I must admit that I loved drinking. It gave me a level of comfort in social situations that I craved, but most of all, it was fun.

The business development work was progressing quite well. Company profits were growing at an increasing pace. This afforded me the ability to begin developing aggressive expansion plans through merger and acquisition along with various joint ventures. The idea was to create an entirely integrated regional healthcare delivery system. This meant combining the hospital with medical groups and health insurance plans. With the many stakeholders that come into play with differing cultures and in many cases conflicting agendas, this challenge would prove to be nothing less than a herculean task. There were no models in place. We were breaking new ground. Nevertheless, we made bold strides toward a truly integrated system and received accolades in several industry journals as well as in the mainstream press. This strategy was risky; however, it was proving to be very successful. With all success comes severe challenges and we were unable to avoid our fair share.

6. The Turning Point

Powerful politicians took issue with the changes that were taking place at their community hospital. Also, the medical community was at odds with our vision of the ever-changing competitive healthcare marketplace. In particular, physicians that held longstanding contracts with the hospital felt that they may be in jeopardy of losing their contracts or suffering income loss. Many employees from management to those on the front lines were not happy with the change in culture. Even members of the board of the hospital felt that they were losing power to the formation of a parent holding company.

We were not making many friends and obviously stepping on many toes in the process. We soon began receiving audits as well as investigations from various governmental agencies such as the IRS, California State Attorney General, and the US Justice Department. Whistleblowers started coming out of the woodwork making specific claims of fraud and abuse. It wasn't long when lawsuits began springing up like weeds in a field. There were many plaintiffs such as community organizations, medical groups, insurance companies and even joint-venture partners. The claims did not come all at once but seemed to build on one another. Many of the complaints seemed ridiculous on the surface, but the governmental agencies ongoing investigations tended to give them all a certain level of creditability.

At first, I was very energetic in defending myself and the company against these outrageous claims. I always prided myself on being on the up-and-up. There was nothing to hide. Even though we were on the cutting edge, I was still careful that we never drifted outside what was called "safe harbors" regarding legality. I kept all the partners and various boards fully informed of the level of their need to know.

Consequently, I was very confident that we would prevail in setting the record straight.

Without realizing it, I had entered into a new phase of work. I began to see that I was no longer spending my work days developing new creative ways of competing in business, but now I was spending the majority of my time looking back and trying to defend my actions. While spending a fair amount of time staying on top of the AG and IRS investigations, I was also knee deep in the discovery process for our first significant lawsuit. We had a topnotch litigator handling this case. I spent close to two years educating my lawyers on every aspect of this case. This was a grueling process for our legal team left no stone unturned. During this time, we prevailed regarding the AG investigation and negotiated a modest settlement with IRS. After nearly two years of discovery on the first suite and hours of deposition, we prevailed at a summary judgment hearing with our lawyers arguing that the plaintiffs did not have legal standing. This was a massive relief after becoming much more concerned about this case as we approached the trial. However, there was little time to relax with another lawsuit queuing up against us from a significant joint-venture partner.

All these lawsuits and investigations were now beginning to take a toll on me. I still had daily job responsibilities that were being neglected. A breakup with one of our significant partners was a significant drag on profitability. Also, legal fees were through the roof, cash flow had turned negative, and board members were getting nervous. High levels of stress were always part of the job, but now for the first time in my career, I was feeling burned out. Work was no longer fun, and I had little to look forward to. I had been a daily drinker for some time now, but I was beginning to discover that I now was looking forward to cocktail hour with a sense of need versus just a well-deserved pleasure. My consumption of alcohol had been creeping up like invisible cancer. Without even noticing, my drinking consumption had nearly doubled in the prior two years. In fact, I was constantly looking forward to getting home from late-night wine and dine business meetings, just to relax at home with a couple of scotches that extended into early morning before bedtime. I still managed to get up for morning management meetings, but it was getting much more difficult.

As we approached the final stages of this next lawsuit, I was wearing down considerably. My several days of deposition were even more grueling in this case. My performance was failing in these depositions and the other side could sense my weakness. This was a difficult case because it was brought by my previous partners and business associates. This was a case where the board voted against a proposed strategic alliance, which I believed was crucial to our ongoing survival. I had presented solid arguments to the board and made my best case for a positive long-term strategic partnership. Due to prejudices by individual board members, the proposal was voted down by a tie-breaking vote. This vote was devastating to our long-term plan, causing us to unwind an agreement with our most important strategic partner. It also brought on our most important lawsuit that would not only prove to be devastating to our corporate goals but also to me personally. This suit was more like a family breaking up in a nasty divorce. I was now fighting with old friends. These were people that I had worked with and trusted. Now, we were pitted against each other as enemies. I never had the same level of confidence in this case as I did with previous legal matters.

At this final phase of trial preparation, both my wife and I realized that my drinking was out of control. I admitted to her that I had a severe problem, but I always had a plan that I could fix it and get my drinking back under control. After all, I had controlled my drinking for nearly forty years. I had been a daily drinker for the better part of the last fifteen years and was able to function just fine. Even though I failed to fix it over and over again, I was able to manage in some way at work. But every time my plan failed at moderating or controlling my drinking, it only got worse. I tried to keep my depression from Cheryl, but she could see that I was failing. I'm sure she was praying a lot for me. She never nagged at me, but always encouraged me to seek help. I remembered that I would pray to God for help, but I had no idea how to pray for at this point I had no personal relationship with God. I had never really asked God for anything. I was always in control, and my trusted self-reliance was my most positive virtue. In fact, I believed that praying to God was foolish. Praying may be useful for those who are weak, but it had no place for one who is self-sufficient and independent like me. That would show weakness. I felt trapped. It seemed nearly impossible to admit that I need help voluntarily. I would probably have to be forced into it.

ACT II-NEW MAN

7. What Happened?

As I was making the morning drive into downtown LA to meet with Dave and the legal team for trial preparation, I had no idea that this would be the day of reckoning. The day that I would come clean with Dave, my lawyer, no less, and admit to my alcoholism. I knew that I had some cleanup work to do regarding several mistakes that I had made under oath during depositions. Also, I was feeling shaky after my typical late night to early morning drinking. I never did get to the point of drinking upon waking, but I did have an uneasy stomach feeling, and my hands would shake while drinking my morning coffee. It was probably deep down into my subconscious that laid dormant a need to be relieved of my mounting anxiety. I just did not want to go there consciously. I avoided it like the plaque. It would probably have to be like an eruption and explode out of me. And, that is precisely what happened as I set in that conference room later that morning preparing for what seemed like my execution.

This day turns out to be a day to remember. It was the beginning of something big, but I had no idea what. It took an eruption within me that put into motion a chain of events that turned my whole life upside down. It was as if there was something in the background that took control. I was no longer in charge.

I felt a sense of relief after making a full admission to Dave that "I can't do it. I need help." That's all it took, a few simple words. But these few simple words had been near impossible for such a proud man as me to utter. But once uttered, there was such relief. As I admitted to Dave that I was an alcoholic and needed help, it was now Dave who was full of anxiety. In a way, I had transferred all my anxiety to him. I had let go, and now Dave had to find a way to deal with something he had never encountered before.

Finally, Dave asked, "Does your doctor know about your drinking?"

"No, he doesn't," I said. "Nobody knows except my wife and now you." So Dave's idea was to have a meeting with my doctor thinking that it is a medical problem. It didn't matter to Dave if it was a medical problem or not; he just needed to unload it onto another professional so that he could carry on with the legal case. And that is what he proceeded to do.

For the first time in my life, I was finally exposed. I had let go of any attempt to hide or run away from the situation. I had come clean with my attorney, my physician, and my boss as we made plans to go forward with the trial. I was not able to do anything about my drinking at that time, but I did have a support team that was sympathetic and provided much-needed medical and emotional support before and during the trial. But the most important thing that happened at this time was the commitment I made to my dear wife. I committed to entering an alcohol treatment program immediately after the trial. Other than me, the one who has had to live the daily emotional pain and suffering was Cheryl. She was always there for me with her encouragement and support while knowing that there was little she could do. It was like watching suicide in slow motion. She suffered immensely while continually doing what little she could to help. What she did do was to protect our precious daughter from seeing her dad going down fast. More importantly, what she always did was to pray to God for the family and me. And it worked!

8. The Miracle

I remember it so well. It was Friday, March 14, 2003. This day was to be the day of my last drink, the day that I would drive myself down PCH to Newport from my home in Long Beach and check in to the alcohol treatment center for a twenty-one-day inpatient program. It had been all planned out in advance. Cheryl and Kendall left early in the morning to spend the weekend at a bridal shower at Cheryl's sister's house north of Bakersfield. Cheryl had explained to Kendall that when they would return home on Sunday, that her dad would be away on an extended business trip for at least a week or so. All I had to do was get to the treatment center for check-in before 5:00 p.m. that evening. I slept in that morning knowing that I wasn't going to work.

I had plenty of time to get ready; hence, I was in no hurry. I figured that I would have a few drinks before check-in since after all this would be my last hurrah. At fifty-five years old, I felt like I had a good run. I began this drinking career at fifteen years old and now forty years later the party was over. This was my forty years of wandering in the wilderness. Realizing that I could never drink again, I felt like life was now over or at least I would never be able to have fun again. It was a horrible feeling, and like all bad feelings, a drink could make it better. Also, I was scared to death of what was going too happened. I was giving up control of my life, and that was extremely uncomfortable. But then again, a few drinks would settle me down. And of course, an alcoholic cannot have just one or a few drinks. After consuming nearly a half bottle of scotch that day, I proceeded down the highway to check-in just before five o'clock. I did, in fact, check-in as planned. After a brief check-in process with a reasonably high alcohol count on the breath analysis, they assigned me a bed and gave me dinner as I met some of the other patients.

While I was getting ready for bed, the buzz began to wear off, so they gave me some medication for sleep. I wasn't able to get much sleep that first night, but it did feel good as I lay in bed for showing the courage to take my first real step to get professional help. I have never had a drink since that day.

Upon awakening the next morning with little sleep, I did feel a bit uncomfortable in this strange new setting. I did not, however, feel any of the typical unpleasant effects of detoxification. I was sure that the medication provided throughout the night for sleeping was helpful. While the other patients were already up and participating in group sessions, the nurses suggested that I stay in bed and get much-needed rest before trying to participate in the program. However, I was anxious to get started. After all, it was Saturday, March 15, 2003, which was my first day of sobriety. I had spent the last forty years wandering in the wilderness, and it was now time to start a new chapter in my life. Just like always, I didn't want to waste any time. My attitude was to jump in and get this thing going. And I did just that.

I took to the program very well. The program combined both the medical clinical approach with the AA twelve-step spiritual program. We were provided the two main books used in the AA program: Big Book of Alcoholics Anonymous (Big Book) and the twelve steps and twelve traditions (twelve-by-twelve). I had no idea what to expect, but I quickly embraced the spiritual concept of the twelve-step program. Since I always had strong desire to know God, I was encouraged with the twelve-step approach of turning to God for help. Mind you before coming in, I had lost all hope and was utterly destitute regarding any personal relationship with God. Sure, I went through the motions in going to church with the family, but I had lost all contact with God. In reality, I had been at war with God for a long time without even knowing it. But now I was beginning to have hope for the first time in a long while.

After completing two weeks of the three-week program, I felt that I was now ready to check out early and return to my principal job. I was doing well and after all the last week was just family week. I was convinced that my family life was right; I was ready to check out and get on with life. The treatment center staff was entirely opposed to any idea of early discharge.

They explained how vital family week was in order complete my treatment program, and adequately bridge the gap in returning home to the family. I tried to explain, to no avail, how supportive my wife was and therefore family week wasn't necessary in my case. They did prevail in convincing me to stay which in retrospect was probably the most important choice that I made early in recovery.

The format of family week was to bring together the patients and their close family members in a group setting to openly forge a truthful and honest relationship between members as we all enter a new life of recovery. The pivotal point of this week came the day when Cheryl and I sat face to face and read our letters in front of the group. The crucial moment came as Cheryl read her letter to me in a very caring and loving tone. The essence of her message to me was very much to the point. In so many words, she merely said that I let her down, she said that I let our daughter down and that I let the whole family down. While these words were crushing to me, my initial thought that flashed through my mind was that . . . *I'm not that bad . . . yeah but . . . look at those people . . . I'm not as bad as them* . . . and after all I've been a good provider for the family . . . the kids are in private school. I was always good at defending myself. I could self-justify and rationalize with the best of them. This thinking was just a flash in my mind, it was my typical response, but then it hit me like a ton of bricks. I realized that I had no defense, she was right, and I was wrong. I broke down with tears streaming down my cheeks. There was no justification; I had failed at the most important things in my life. My accomplishments were not important, I had failed as a husband and father, and my pride had been shattered. The idea that I had let my daughter down was devastating to me. My daughter Kendall met everything to me. I felt sick to my stomach. The emotional pain was piercing. I remember so clearly thinking that some way, somehow I had to change my ways. But I had no idea how I could do this. It would take a miracle. In my thoughts, it was like I suddenly went into a silent prayer asking God for a second chance. I'll do anything to make good.

9. The "Bad News–Good News" Story

The AA program is "bad news-good news" story. The good news is the newfounded hope and the promise of a new life. But the bad news is as stated in the twelve-by-twelve, which says, "In every case, pain had been the price of admission into a new life. But this admission price had purchased more than we expected. It brought a measure of humility, which we soon discovered to be a healer of pain. We began to fear pain less, and desire humility more than ever."

With humility, I changed my attitude toward God. As the twelve-by-twelve goes on to say, "Of myself I am nothing, the Father Doeth the works' began to carry bright promise and meaning." The program says that in every case pain is the price and humility is the healer of pain. My experience during family week was precisely this. The pain was piercing, and the humility was extraordinary. I don't believe that I had ever experienced this level of emotional pain and humility before. I soon discovered that humility is the foundation of all the twelve steps as well as coming to the foot of the Cross.

I didn't know it at the time, but that very moment when I quit the argument, the self-justification, and looked to God for help, everything changed. The family week experience was truly humbling, and it provided relief from the pain. To this day, I believe that this was when God showed up in my life. The very next day before checking out of the treatment center, I met my AA sponsor, Walt. Walt was perfect sponsor for me. He had helped a lot of guys; he was a few years older and was even alum of the same university where I graduated. He immediately laid out a substantial program of recovery for me, and I was on my way of a beautiful journey of a lifetime.

When I returned home and went back to work, life would never be the same again. I now knew that my AA recovery program had to be first in my life. God was to be first before family, work, and everything else. I realized that at my age, I needed to get this thing or die. Therefore, I had no choice but to go all in. This new life also met that I could no longer go back to that high-pressure job of mine. My resignation would mean a considerable drop in income, but my life was more important to my family and me than any material concerns. Fortunately, we had sizeable savings along with some deferred compensation that could hold us over until I would be able to reestablish myself in some other line of business. The most important thing was that I had to focus on my recovery above everything else.

Upon my return to the office, I immediately met with my boss, Alan, to offer my resignation. I wasn't obligated to resign, but I do believe that Alan had anticipated this eventuality. As I submitted my resignation, Alan suggested that we step back and take another look at the situation. Alan understood my position well and knew that there was no way that I would continue with the workload and level of responsibility that had driven me to my despair. However, he also knew full well that he and the company needed me for at least a couple more years. There was still more litigation on the horizon, and Alan also needed my help to transition the organization in downsizing. He offered a couple of alternatives, but I only listened to the first option before agreeing. The first offer seemed fair enough for me to accept and get on. To be so accepting was unlike me, for I would typically consider all my options and negotiate the best deal possible.

I realized then that something was already different about me as if God had taken charge and I was okay with it. I had lost my fear and had a definite feeling of being protected. I felt as if I had no time for negotiation; I just wanted to get on with my new life. The plan was for me to play an advisory role for the corporation and be available for any of the upcoming lawsuits. My compensation would be reduced, but I would be provided health benefits for two years and provided the freedom to engage fully in my new recovery program.

I thought my recovery program was going to be difficult. After all, it is a tiny percentage of alcoholics that stay sober for a year. Most relapse within months. Whatever the case, the odds are not good. But the good news was that I didn't have to do this on my own. I had my sponsor, my meetings, my family, and many others who were all very supportive. The basic recovery plan consists of attending ninety AA meetings in ninety days and working the twelve steps with the guidance of my sponsor. And of course, continue meetings for a lifetime. At first, it was a struggle to go to meetings every day, but it wasn't long before I looked forward to meetings. I learned to listen, and I also began to enjoy sharing my own experience, strength, and hope at the meetings. The fellowship in AA was so much more than I ever thought. I found honesty, love, and most importantly hope. Most everyone in AA meetings is there for not only their own needs but also to help others. There is a lot of laughter, but it is also about the serious business of life and death. But the most crucial part of the program is working the twelve steps with a sponsor.

It took about one year to go through all twelve steps rigorously and honestly. As Bill W. says in his story in the Big Book,

"Simple but not easy; a price has to be paid. It meant the destruction of self-centeredness." He goes on to say, "I must turn in all things to the Father of Light who presides over us all." Bill W. also said that "These were revolutionary and drastic proposals, but the moment I fully accepted them, the effect was electric."

Before I got to AA, I thought that drinking was the source of all my problems. But I learn in AA that alcohol is just the symptom, and the root of the problem is self-centered fear. I drank to cover up my fears. Drinking became my solution. But like most pain medication, it is a short-term remedy. Most physicians well explain that we should not treat symptoms. Only after diagnosis is determined, should a treatment plan be prescribed.

The first step states, "We admitted we were powerless over alcohol—that our lives had become unmanageable." The program starts with the word "we," which suggests that I don't need to make this journey by myself. Also, this step establishes that we must define the problem. The next eleven steps provide the solution. The second step states, "Coming to believe in a power greater than ourselves could restore us to sanity." The twelve-step solution is all about turning to God. The Big Book talks about abandoning yourself to God because it is only by His grace that the miracle of sobriety can happen.

But it was the third step that opened the door to the new life. The third step states, "Made a decision to turn our will and our lives over to the care of God *as we understand Him*." Because of being in a state of total desperation, the first two steps were taken without question. It was as if I did not have a choice to admit that I was powerless and that it would take a power greater than me to recover from this deadly illness. But at step 3, I was at a fork in the road, and now I had to take action. At this step, I was being asked to give up control of my own life and turn it over to God. Bill W. had said that this program is simple but not easy.

But the third step is not only not easy, but next to impossible. I had lived my adult life striving to be self-sufficient and proud of it. Now I'm told that the idea that pride, self-sufficiency, and being self-reliant was the root of the problem. I told my sponsor that I didn't know how a self-willed control freak like me can honestly take this step. It didn't seem possible. My sponsor explained that all this step asks of me is to make a decision. He went on to ask, "Aren't you a decision maker in your job? Don't you make major decisions that commit you and your organization on a regular basis?" The answer became apparent as I thought it through.

Yes, I can make a decision. I was at a fork in the road, and a choice had to be made. In looking back, this was indeed the most significant decision of my life. The options of either continuing down the road of the self-centered life or turning to this new path of a God-centered life had to be made. It was that simple; either I'm all in, or I'm not, what was my choice to be. I made the ultimate commitment; I'm all in! I chose God, and again everything then changed. Suddenly, the idea of giving up control of my life to the care of God didn't seem so difficult. I didn't realize it at the time, what I see today—that God was doing for me what I could not do for myself.

Making the decision was my total surrender. At this point, I was about two months into my twelve-step work when I started to care about going to church for worship and giving thanksgiving to God. I had been given a gift, and I was filled with gratitude. Along with my "AA Daily Reflections" reading, I began a daily reading of the biblical devotional "My Utmost for His Highest" by Oswald Chambers. I read C. S. Lewis's book, *Mere Christianity*, which had a significant impact on me. This book helped me draw a strong parallel between the Christian faith and the twelve steps of AA. I was now brought to reading scripture along with other Christian literature while at the same time continuing my study of the AA literature and working the twelve-step program. I was also baptized, and it wasn't long before I joined Bible study fellowships.

It is by the grace of a loving God that I am sober today. By His amazing grace, I have been reborn. Today I am child of God the Father and adopted into His Kingdom. Death to the self-centered life and arisen in the God-centered life. Glory be to God! This is my amazing AA story that transforms life from the bondage of self to a new truth that will set you free. The twelve-step program is not a religious program, but it is based on Christian biblical principles. Also, Christianity is not a religion as well. Christianity is a revelation of God through a personal relationship with Jesus Christ. As C. S. Lewis said, "Believing in Christianity is like believing in the rising sun, it is not simply that you can see it, but by it, you can see everything else." This is amazing grace for I once was blind, but now I see.

10. The New Life

As a recovering alcoholic, my courage, strength, and hope are bolstered by relying on both the fellowship of the twelve-step program and the Gospel of Jesus Christ. I have seen Anglican priests, and other men of the cloth get sober in Alcoholics Anonymous. Men of God often need more than religion and church to get them sober. Alcoholics need the AA fellowship including God and the twelve-step program. For me, the twelve-step program is an excellent instruction manual for the good news of the Gospel. The good news of the twelve-step program is its principle focus on having a spiritual awakening and being filled with the spirit of God. God's grace is amazing. We cannot explain how grace works. There may not be an adequate explanation, but there is a formulation; it's the twelve steps of Alcoholics Anonymous and the Gospel of Jesus Christ.

The rest of the story is the good news. This new life is not perfect by any means. We will always have trials and tribulations. But my trials are now cornerstones for spiritual growth. With God, I have a new courage, strength, and hope no matter what the difficulties. Faith and courage go together. By faith, we are encouraged and gain Courage that empowers us to act in favor of what we believe. The Big Book says, "All men of faith have courage." The promises of the Big Book have come true: "We will be amazed before we are halfway through. We are going to know a new freedom and a new happiness . . . Our whole attitude and outlook on life will change . . . We suddenly realized that God is doing for us what we could not do for ourselves." Having had a spiritual awakening as the result of these steps, God has entered my heart and soul. Once God invaded my heart and grabbed on, He never let go. He is the peace, hope, freedom and most of all, love. Love is now winning out over fear. It's an inside job. This game of life has been rigged from the beginning and . . . God won! The only chance I had was absolute and total surrender! I quit the argument and joined His side.

What is this new life? Three attributes of my life underwent a significant change of attitude, behavior, and values, as follows:

1. New attitude and outlook—gratitude vs. entitlement
2. New behavior—doing the right thing vs. what I can get away with

3. New values—love of God and His fellow man vs. love of self

Today and every day, I ask God to help me with five areas of my life:

1. Live in the present, one day at a time: don't regret the past or worry about the future. I used to continually project most everything out into the future and worry about it. Today, I replace worry with prayer. It is only in the present state that I can connect to my infinite God.
2. An attitude of gratitude: always gives glory to God for He provides everything.
3. Trust God by abandoning myself to Him (third step)

    a) Surrender to the process (my job).
    b) Let go and give up the results to Him (His job)

4. Love my fellows: look for the good in the sinner and not sin in the saint. Be of service, be teachable, forgiving and praise others.
5. Live life on its terms: accepts this sinful world as it is, as He did, not as I would have it.

Before checking into the treatment center, I thought life was over. I just could not imagine not drinking for the rest of my life. But the last fifteen years of my sobriety have been the best years of my life. By living one day at a time, turning to God daily, keeping my house clean and giving freely, my life has taken on a real purpose of being of use to Him. A complete change has taken place in the way that I approach life. I used to avoid difficult situations where today I take on challenges with a sense of gratitude. Instead of wanting to run away from problems via the bottle, I seek God and the fellowship for a solution.

Today, I attend AA meetings daily, sponsor fellow alcoholics, carry the message on AA panels in treatment centers and jails, participate in Bible study fellowships, and share my story wherever it may encourage. I do these things today not because I ought to, but because I want. This is true freedom. My wife and I have developed a small professional nationwide real-estate business, which provides us the ability to travel the country. My focus in the company is not so much to possess but to serve.

My relationship with my wife continues to grow stronger. Cheryl has been my best supporter. God has used her to save me. She is not only the love of my life, but we are the best of friends and spend a lot of time together. Cheryl is not just a beautiful wife, but also an excellent grandmother and we both enjoy spending time with our grandkids. My love for my miracle baby, Kendall, could not be greater for she has a father that would do anything for her. And I know that she has great love for her dad. After all, Kendall's husband, Edsel, has the same birth date as I, only forty years later. I feel honored when Kendall claims that she married a man much like her father. I just hope that my son-in-law feels the same. As of the date of this writing our miracle baby, Kendall has given birth to her first baby, Colette. Another miracle! Our miracle baby, Kendall (she is thirty years of age as of this writing) giving birth to our miracle grandbaby, Colette. Kendall is now pregnant with her second baby girl named Margot. What a blessing. Life doesn't get much better than this.

Both Trent and Amy stay very close to me as well. Trent often looks to me for advice on some of his business opportunities. Trent exhibits trust in me by seeking my help and support in both his good and bad times. Amy married a wonderful man, Chris, who is a Christian and a Ventura County sheriff. They have four of our six grandchildren today. Trent has not yet married but is growing in faith and doing well in business. Kendall is director of Children's Ministry at their church and Edsel, a wonderful husband and devoted Christian, has completed his PhD with honors and is in the process of finishing medical school. The relationship with my wife Cheryl and all my kids including the grandkids are better than I could have ever imagined. Some of them even seek my counsel on occasion and look to me for guidance.

When asked, what is the fundamental difference of my life today from what it was before; my reply is simply—"I don't have to prove myself anymore." I have given up all pretenses. I no longer need to hide behind my façade which created so many of my fears. Today I have but one master—Almighty God. Before, I had many masters. Even though I would not admit it, I had all the idols of wealth, fame and/or prestige and a whole lot of pride. But today, with my only master being my God, there is little fear, worry or need to prove myself. Godly men glorify God, but Godless men glorify self. Scripture talks about how we cannot serve two masters. The Bible also says, "I care little if I am judged by you or by any human court; indeed, I do not even judge myself" (1 Corinthians 4:3). God is my owner by creation and also my owner by right of purchase. I was bought at a price . . . the precious blood of Jesus Christ. With God as my only master, the hidden treasure is revealed. As the Big Book states in chapter 2, there is a solution, "The great fact is just this and nothing less: That we have had deep and effective spiritual experiences which have revolutionized our attitude toward life, toward our fellows and toward God's universe. The central fact of lives today is the absolute certainty that our Creator has entered into our hearts and lives in a way which is indeed miraculous. He has commenced to accomplish those things for us which we could never do by ourselves."

Truly amazing!

PS: To the newcomers; all this talk of miracles, gifts from God, amazing grace, may all seem so foolish. That is what I thought at first. I pray that like me you will receive the gift of desperation and quit the argument—God won; it's *finished!* So join us on the road of happy destiny. May God bless you . . . (Donald C. Wes).

CHAPTER II

The Problem: Act of War Man's Enmity toward God

> "If God were not so holy,
> and we were not so sinful,
> perhaps we could get along."
>
> —R. C. Sproul

As I described in "My Story," I thought drinking was the source of my all my problems. But I soon learned in recovery, that drinking was but a symptom and the root cause of the problem was self-centered fear. I drank to cover up my fears. I had worked my whole life to be self-sufficient and independent. I saw it as a virtue to be ambitious and self-reliant. I took great pride in this attribute. I did not need your help, thank you very much. In fact, I didn't even need God's help. I claimed to believe in God, but I failed to put my trust in Him. I only trusted myself and thought that prayer was foolish. Prayer was good for the weak, but not for the strong, "pull yourself up by the boot straps" type of man that I was. So I was more than unsettled to discover that what I considered to be my primary virtue in life was the cause of my problem, namely pride.

Before any solution can be developed, a clear definition of the problem must be determined. The problem of the alcoholic is the same as all humankind which is described clearly in the first book of the Bible. The book of Genesis explains how Adam and Eve sadly decide that they could live better on their own without God. The Bible describes from the beginning that humankind has inherited this self-centeredness from Adam. We all live in a fallen world and need a Savior.

In the book of Romans 3, Paul summarizes God's diagnosis of every person's lack of spiritual health. Adam and Eve's contagion spread spiritual death through sin and therefore we all receive God's condemnation. In Romans 3:10–11 Paul says, "There is no one righteous, not even one; there is no one who understands; there is no one who seeks God." Paul makes clear that we are all alike concerning sin. Therefore, we are all subject to the wrath of God and will be judged accordingly. We have no defense, and there is no exception, no human-made solution, no pretense, and no denying or justification. We are all guilty.

The Bible speaks about man's rebellion against God and how the world has rejected God, therefore setting a course that leads us to the darker side and further from God. Nothing about God appeals to man or woman who denies God. In Fact, everything about God is objectionable to humankind. First of all, we want to be in control of our own lives. We reject God's sovereignty. Therefore, we want to be free to practice our desires and not be confined by God's holiness and continue to do whatever we can get away with. Also, we don't like the idea that God knows everything. We feel that God is intrusive which causes us to cover up and hide from God. Finally, God is too much a hard-liner. He does not bend to our particular circumstances. Everything is black or white with no compromises. The truth is that the natural condition of humankind is not only a dislike for God but an actual hatred toward our creator. This enmity toward God has caused an outright declaration of war.

The result of this war against God is that people become foolish in regards to their morality and spirituality. This human rebellion exists in spite of the fact that God has made clear through creation that He is all powerful. The revelation of God in nature is referred to as "general revelation." The evidence of God's power through general revelation is available to everyone; hence there is no excuse for disregarding God's power and authority. The truth is that without God, human beings are left with an inadequate understanding and spiritual thinking that is incapable of seeing the light and therefore drifts into darkness. The problem is the human being is oblivious to its predicament. The Big Book defines the problem of alcoholism as a spiritual malady. As the Big Book says, "So our troubles, we think, are basically of our own making. They arise out of ourselves, and the alcoholic is an extreme example of self-will run riot, though he usually doesn't think so." We are neither aware nor willing to admit our predicament. This total blindness to our arrogance is what worsens our spiritual depravity. Our wrong thinking creates the illusion that we are just fine on our own. This thinking is evidence of a lost and broken condition which has no chance for righteousness. Hence, Paul claims that "There is no one righteous . . . no one does good, not even one" (Romans 3:10–11).

If we are unable to grasp the problem that humankind is born with a spiritual depravity, we cannot understand ourselves, our fellows, or the world we live in. And we certainly cannot understand the Christian faith or make any sense out of the Bible. And it is the Bible that is the source of truth that brings to light the problem of human sin and our prideful self-centeredness. The Bible provides the answer to the problem of human sin, and unless we clearly understand the problem, we will keep missing the point of what the Bible is saying. Hence, the problem is further complicated. Without recognizing our predicament, we are not capable of seeing the solution of the good news of the gospel. We are unable to see the message of the Gospel of a loving God providing a pathway to salvation through Christ Jesus.

The depraved mind thinks very highly of itself. This prideful nature claims to be wise with superior knowledge and intellect. The prideful man develops a hardened heart and rejects the truth about God as foolishness. But in reality, the Bible claims to deny God is to have a foolish heart. Humankind's intellectual foolishness even goes so far as to claim that there is no God. "The fool says in his heart, 'There is no God.' They are corrupt, their deeds are vile; there is no one who does good" (Psalms 14:1). And where there is an acceptance of a God, we deny the true God and invoke false Gods with substitute religions. Humanity's rebellion against God is the cause of God's wrath. Hence, all out warfare!

We are enemies of God. Until we surrender, we are powerless, ungodly sinners and yet we wage war against almighty God. We oppose God's sovereignty and deny that we belong to Him. We are defiant and disobedient to His law. As God's enemies, we oppose His ways. If we were able, we would have assaulted and destroyed Him as was done on the cross. We are all guilty of the attempted destruction of Christ on the cross. The Bible clearly portrays a universe at war. C. S. Lewis describes it as "a civil war, a rebellion, and that we are living in a part of the universe occupied by the rebel." Lewis goes on to say that we think we could "be like gods"—could set up on our own . . . apart from God. And out of that hopeless attempt has come nearly all that we call human history—money, poverty, ambition, war, prostitution, classes, empires, slavery—the long terrible story of man trying to find something other than God which will make him happy." Lewis paints a dreadful picture of humanity, but it is the truth. Our problem is that our pride obscures the truth. But the truth will set you free.

Therefore, with no excuse, the human condition has no escape from eternal condemnation, except through God Himself. With a God given free will, one would think that man could make a reasoned choice. We do have free will, but the Bible says that we are a slave to sin. The tragedy for humankind is that our free will has been corrupted by our need for self-glorification. This perversion continues to grow in ungodly ways. Like the alcoholic, the harder we try to control our addiction, the worse it gets. The Bible says that we are slaves to sin and that we are in a state of death. Sin is very deceitful. Sin promises freedom, but all who serve sin find themselves in bondage to self. All people serve someone, either sin or God. When we rebel against God, we offer ourselves as a slave to ever-increasing depravity. Our transgressions always lead to increased slavery and ultimately to spiritual death. There is no middle ground. Our condemnation continually increases with no apparent way out.

For many, the answer to our predicament is found in religion. Since religion does speak of sin as it is defined by the law. The law actually reveals what sin is. We recognize our wrongdoing when we violate God's law. Until we grasp that we have broken God's law, we do not see our moral failures as offences against God. Knowing the law is helpful, but it is not a cure all. The reason being is that none of us are capable of obeying the law. Hence, we resort to self-justification when we fall short in our obedience. With this need to self-justify, we are in a constant state of believing that "I'm not that bad."

We continue to compare ourselves to others when justifying our misdeeds or excusing ourselves by blaming others. Left to our own thinking, none of us believe we are sinners. The question is what is behind the "mask" of our deception. This "mask of deception" is nothing but a cover-up. Since we are unable to own up to our failures, we lie to ourselves, God and everyone else. Hence, we are blind to the truth. Even in religion, we will role play producing a self-righteous state of mind. The Bible makes this clear in Psalm 36:2, "In their own eyes they flatter themselves too much to detect or hate their sin." In "My Story," it was when I finally realized that my wife was right and I was wrong . . . and I quite the argument and self-justification . . . then and only then did God show up. But as long as I held on to the "big lie," the "death spiral" continued out of control.

God's law does not only reveal sin, but it also provokes sin. It is human nature to resent commandments. It is okay to make suggestions about our behavior, but by no means make direct demands or command. The Big Book goes to great lengths to explain all the twelve-step principles as suggestions vs. commandments. An alcoholic with a "self-will run riot" condition will rarely be open to accepting directives. Hence, the law agitates anger and causes rebellion. When the law says "you shall not . . ." we immediately want to do the prohibited thing. Therefore, the law actually provokes our wicked ways.

The heart of the problem is that the focus of the nature of man is all about itself. This is not an isolated problem; it is universal. Without recognizing it, the unbelieving mind sets itself up as God himself. By definition, self-reliance is discarding God and putting ourselves in his place. Again, we perpetuate a hostile attitude toward the true God. Our basic instinctive nature is to please ourselves. We are unable to obey God's law. Enmity toward God is a built-in default measure that we cannot avoid. The Bible says in Ephesians 2:1, "You were dead in your transgressions and sins." We were not just sick but terminally ill. We were dead spiritually.

The Bible makes clear that every human being is born spiritually dead with a prejudice toward sin, inherited from Adam. But the New Testament gives us the Good News of the Gospel where God has provided us the "Way, the Truth and the Life" (John 14:6) through His Son, Jesus Christ, which is our only hope. The twelve steps takes us step by step to a spiritual awakening and the promise that only God can restore us to sobriety and a life of recovery. The Big Book says, "First of all, we had to quit playing God. It didn't work . . . God was going to be our director. He is the Principle; we are His agents." The twelve steps drives home the message that we are powerless over managing our own lives and that only God can restore us to a life of recovery if He were sought.

Both the Bible and the Big Book portray a "bad news—good news" story. According to the twelve steps, "In every case, pain is the price of admission to a new life . . . it brought a measure of humility, which we soon discovered to be a healer of pain." In other words, the bad news of pain and suffering must be endured as an admission price to receive the good news of a new life. In the Bible, Romans 3:10 speaks about spiritual death through sin is what brings upon us God's condemnation and in Romans 8:18 Paul links suffering and glory.

Paul says, "I consider that our present sufferings are not worth comparing with the glory that will be reveled in us." We must first suffer before we receive glory. We must suffer through affliction that takes us to the end of ourselves and forces us to rely on our savior. First go through the Cross, and then receive glory. In Romans 8:1–2, Paul says, "There is therefore now no condemnation for those who are in Jesus Christ. For the law of the Spirit of life has set you free in Jesus Christ . . ." Here again, we have the "bad news–good news" story.

This chapter is the "bad news" story. The rest of the story is how the promises of the Twelve Steps of Alcoholics Anonymous reveal the good news of the Gospel of Jesus Christ. Now that we have a well-defined problem, we are ready to begin our journey in the solution. Since our problem is all about a spiritual death, the solution is all about a spiritual awakening. In the next chapter, we will begin our new journey of truth by summarizing the pathway to a new life. This pathway to truth culminates in a life "reborn" through a spiritual awakening revealing the Gospel of Jesus Christ.

CHAPTER III

The New Life Journey:
Pathway to Truth

Having clearly defined the problem, we are now ready to seek a solution. The problem is defined as a powerless and unmanageable life as a result of our rebellion against God. As we discover that a godless life does not end well, we become willing to venture out on a new journey that is focused on seeking the truth. This chapter provides a high-level view that map out our journey, while the chapters that follow will take us through a step-by-step action plan. The Big Book summarizes the twelve steps as follows: "Abandon yourself to God, as you understand God. Admit your faults to Him and to your fellows. Clear away the wreckage of your past. Give freely of what you find and join us. We shall be with you in the Fellowship of the Spirit, and you will surely meet some of us as you trudge the Road of Happy Destiny."

The Cliff Notes of the twelve steps are the following: trust God, clean house, and help others. These Cliff Notes are helpful guideposts for both working through the twelve steps or our pilgrimage through the gospel. Venturing out on this journey is a risky proposition, but the rewards far outweigh the risk. In fact, this is the journey of lifetime. This is a pilgrimage that will provide the key to your life. It is never too late to start. So let's begin!

1. Comfort vs. Truth

The pathway to the truth is not a not a comfortable endeavor and shall always be a work in progress, for it is a lifetime journey. There is no ultimate destination; however, our pride seeks out a comfortable destination, while our soul seeks the journey. But as C. S. Lewis says, comfort is not something that you can seek out. He says, "If we seek comfort, we will never find the truth; but if we seek the truth, we will receive comfort along the way." The quest for truth has four essential elements to consider in our journey along its pathway, which are: (1) surrender, (2) repentance, (3) forgiveness, and (4) love. Each of these essential elements challenges our pride, fills us with fear and pushes us out of our comfort zone. However, before any journey can begin along any pathway, there must be a perceived need before we venture out. The human condition will not even try to venture out as long as all seems well. If one feels comfortable where they are at, then there is no need to get up and leave.

This truth journey is not only difficult, but it is the most important journey of our life. It threatens our very nature of prideful self-centeredness. The question is always why would we step out of our comfort zone and subject ourselves to the fear of failure? In every case, we must be provoked. Scripture commands us to rend our hearts, but they are naturally as hard as marble; how then, can this be done? We must go to Calvary. But true faith is too humbling, too heart-searching, and too thorough for the tastes of people of the flesh; they prefer an easier way that is worldlier. For the alcoholic, the twelve-by-twelve says, "In every case, pain had been the price of admission into a new life. But this admission price had purchased more than we expected. It brought a measure of humility, which we soon discovered to be a healer of pain."

Our natural instincts are to run away from pain and difficulties. We drink for comfort. Alcohol takes the edge off and reduces our social anxiety. Escape via the bottle became our solution. But then again, this is a temporary solution that only deals with the symptom vs. the root of the problem which is self-centered fear. The alcoholic looks more and more to the drink for his comfort and the only solution he knows. This path leads to only one place, total despair. For most alcoholics, it takes many years for our drinking habit to progress to that near fatal dead end road. It takes hitting bottom. The twelve-by-twelve clearly explains why the alcoholic must hit bottom first. The twelve-by-twelve says, "The answer is that few people will sincerely try to practice the AA program unless they have hit bottom." Step 1 goes on to say, "Who wishes to be rigorously honest and tolerant? Who wants to confess his faults to another and make restitution for harm done? Who cares anything about a Higher Power, let alone meditation and prayer? Who wants to sacrifice time and energy in trying to carry AA's message to the next sufferer? No, the average alcoholic, self-centered in the extreme, doesn't care for this prospect—unless he has to do these things in order to stay alive himself."

Whatever the case, the human condition which naturally seeks comfort, hinders our search for a new way out until our predicament causes sufficient pain that we reach a state of desperation. The alcoholic receives this gift of desperation which is driven by his own self-imposed crises to a state of total despair.

But all godless people will experience their own cross to bear at some point in life. As C. S. Lewis states, "Pain insists upon being attended to. God whispers to us in our pleasures, speaks in our conscience, but shouts in our pains: it is His megaphone to rouse a deaf world."

Unlike the alcoholic, many people may be able to cover it up with more acceptable means such as their work, power, prestige, shopping, prescription drugs, etc. The alcoholic is driven by flat out survival from a fatal condition and in many cases, this is not sufficient. The Bible makes a clear link between suffering and glory. It takes enough suffering to bring us to the end of ourselves for us to turn to our Savior. First comes suffering and then comes glory. The Bible says that suffering is unavoidable. Paul says in Romans 8:17, "We suffer with Christ that we may also be glorified with him." But only if we are suffering from sufficient pain and reach a state of total desperation, can we take the first step: surrender.

2. Surrender

Surrender is not something that comes naturally to anyone. Scripture talks about surrendering all our pretense or deceit. Our Lord does not ask us for our goodness, honesty, or our efforts to do better. All He asks for are our real sins. That is all He wants and that is all we have to offer. What He gives us in exchange is real solid righteousness. But we must surrender all pretenses that we are anything, and give up all our claims that we are worthy. We must be ready to be identified with the death of Jesus Christ. Scripture claims that there is only one God that is trustworthy! We need to discard our entire worldly god's of money, people, and most of all ourselves (false pride). We must place all our trust in the one true God, our heavenly Father as revealed in His Son Jesus Christ.

How do we come to trust in God? First, we must have no doubt about our need. Then secondly, we are so desperate that our pride is stripped from us and we cry out. As we desperately face our need, we come to an end of ourselves. We face up to the fact that we are dead! We are blind! But suddenly, we can see . . . all in the moment when we cry out. At this point, we have turned our will and life over to God without realizing it. This is the beginning. The most profound thing in a person is his will, not sin. The will is the essential element in God's creation of human beings. Scripture says that sin is a perverse nature that entered into the human condition through Adam. If we are to be "born again," the source of the will is Almighty God.

The first step in the twelve-step program asks us to admit that we are powerless over alcohol and our life is unmanageable. The only time alcohol is mentioned is in the first step and it could easily be replaced with the word "sin." This first step is definitely a surrender step, that we can't do it on our own. The admission of powerlessness and the acceptance that we cannot do it on our own is essential to the twelve-step program.

Then the second step provides the hope that we need by stating "Came to believe in a Power greater than ourselves could restore us to sanity." On the surface step 2 doesn't seem so difficult, for many of us claim to believe in some form of God, but most of us don't believe we are insane. We cling to the idea that we can control our drinking and therefore this thinking is perfectly sane even though we fail over and over again at controlling our drinking. One definition of "insanity" is doing the same thing over and over again expecting different results. We need to realize that we can't fix what is in our head with what is in our head. We need a power that comes from outside of us.

But the program of AA is a program of action and the first action step is step 3, the ultimate surrender. The action is making a decision. This is the greatest decision of a lifetime. Step 3 states, "Made a decision to turn our will and our lives over to the care of God *as we understand Him*." This is the most difficult step to make. In fact, it is so difficult that it is virtually impossible to do without God's help. That is why step 3 simply asks us to make a decision. By definition, a decision means a "determination" to commit oneself or "conclusion" regarding direction. Once we have decided, we are committed or as poker player may say, "I'm all in." There is no going back.

This is the heartfelt attitude that one must have when making the ultimate surrender. With this decision, we are placing total trust on this choice; trust in God. As described in "My Story," it happened when I quite the argument and stopped trying to justify my behavior. It was at the moment when my wife said that I had let her down and after trying to justify myself, I was struck by God. Like Saul on the road to Damascus, God was asking me why I was persecuting Him. Stubbornness and self-will will always stab Jesus. Whenever, we are hardheaded and self-willed and set on our own ways, we are hurting God. So we must place our trust in God. Throughout scripture, God asks us to put our trust in Him. When we walk on God's path of trust, we live above our circumstances. We begin to look to God before making our choices and we leave the results in His hands, hence we need not worry. The Big Book asks us to think well before taking this step making sure we were ready; "that we could at last abandon ourselves utterly to Him."

3. Repentance

Having made the ultimate surrender, the Big Book suggests that we next launch into vigorous action of personal housekeeping, which many of us had never attempted. This brings us to the second essential element in our quest for truth, which is repentance. The Big Book also suggests that even though our total surrender was a crucial step, it may have little permanent effect unless at once it is followed by repentance or by a strenuous effort to face, and to be rid of, the things in ourselves which had been blocking us. Steps 4 and 5 of the Big Book suggest that we take a searching and fearless moral inventory of ourselves and admit our faults to God and our fellows.

Repentance means that we must first recognize our sins and then confess our sins not only to God but also another human being. Scripture says in James 5:16, "Confess your sins to each other and pray for each other so that you may be healed." It does not say that we must confess our sins to a priest. Also, it does not say that we confess our sins to God only. The confession is to God, but having a fellow as witness helps us to be honest. As described in "My Story," the capacity to be honest with myself was severely lacking. I was able to self-justify or self-deceive with the best of them. The idea of repentance is to come clean, so honesty is paramount. But our natural pride blinds us to the truth. We are unable to see ourselves as we really are. Again, we cannot do this on our own. We need help from God and our fellows to come clean. My nature claims that I'm not that bad, in fact I'm pretty darn good compared to those other people. So the first step in repentance is to recognize the seriousness of our sinful nature.

Therefore, we need to gain knowledge of sin, which means an awareness of one's own quilt, perversity, uncleanness, and lack of moral purpose as seen by God. Scripture makes it clear that we are not alone, for we are all sinners. As stated earlier, in Chapter II, we have all inherited a nature of total depravity from Adam. Scripture says, "No one is righteous—not even one. No one is truly wise; no one is seeking God. All have turned away; all have become useless" (Romans 3:10–12). We are all made the same—both good and bad.

Repentance is confessing our self-reliance and all those other things that we rely on for our hope and security other than God—all those things that we are trying to find other than God, which will make us happy. Therefore, we must stop rationalizing our sins and admit the truth—come clean. In step 5 we stop the struggle and admit our wrongs. We get honest with God and ourselves and come clean. We quit the argument, the lie, the excuses, and the bargain. We finally admit that we are guilty as charged.

In Scripture, we take our sins to the Cross. The gospel is the good news that God sent his Son Jesus Christ to die on the cross for our sins and bear the penalty that we deserved. We are no longer viewed as being guilty for our sins. We have been cleansed by the blood of Christ. As Christ hangs on the cross, He says, "Father, forgive them, for they know not what they do." Christ is not spared by the Father for He died for our sins and we are forgiven. There is no real freedom without repentance and confession. We receive a tremendous relief when we finally give up the weight of our lies and excuses. The foundation of Christianity is repentance. Oswald Chambers explained it best in his classic devotional book Utmost for His Highest: "That the entrance into the kingdom of God is through the sharp, sudden pains of repentance colliding with man's respectable goodness."

Then the Holy Spirit, who produces these struggles, begins the formation of the Son of God in the person's life. This is a gift from God. This new life will reveal itself in conscious repentance followed by unconscious holiness, never the other way around." The Bible says that we were "born again" and the Big Book says that, "We were reborn." Whatever the case, there is a new freedom, forgiveness, hope, and joy.

4. Forgiveness

The next essential element in our quest for truth is forgiveness. By the grace of God we have been forgiven of our sins therefore, we must forgive. Scripture says that we must forgive to be forgiven. As Jesus Christ states in the Lord's Prayer, "Forgive us our trespasses as we forgive those who trespass against us." Having received God's mercy, grace and forgiveness, we are no longer our own. We have been purchased at a price. Therefore we are owned by God. "Do you not know that your body is a temple of the Holy Spirit, who is in you, whom you have received from God?" (1 Corinthians 6:19). Your time, money and talents are not your own but God's. When we realize that we don't deserve God's mercy, then how can we withhold mercy for another? Therefore we can no longer cling to our rights and refuse to forgive. Since God has forgiven us, we ask God to give us His heart and His mind. By God's grace we are born again into a new life and this sanctifying work is carried on in two ways: (1) lust of the flesh is subdued and (2) the life of God within us comes alive like a well of water springing up into everlasting life. What springs up from this well is a whole new attitude of gratitude which strips us of our pride and brings on a measure of humility.

Genuine humility cannot be attained by avoiding pride; it can only be attained by discovering gratitude.

In steps 6 and 7, we are entirely ready and we humbly ask God to remove our shortcomings. These steps discuss an honest willingness and humility to ask God to purify us through the sanctification process. Scripture ask us if we are willing to let Jesus to become sanctification to us, and to let His life be exhibited in our human flesh. (See 1 Corinthians 1:30.) We receive Jesus Christ by absolute, unquestioning faith to become sanctification for us and the great miracle of the atonement of Jesus Christ will become real in our lives. Steps 6 and 7 are regarded as the "hinge" steps of the twelve-step program. The first five steps deal with removing the obstacles that have prevented us from a loving relationship with God. The last five steps provide a process for repairing our relationship with both God and our fellows. By God's grace we become eternally grateful for our new God-centered life. With this God given gratitude, it brought a measure of humility, which we discovered to be a healer of pain. The Big Book says that "We began to fear pain less, and desire humility more than ever . . . of myself I am nothing, the Father Doeth the works." The whole emphasis of step 7 is humility. As the Big Book says, "This is where we make the change in our attitude which permits us, with humility as our guide, to move out from ourselves toward others and toward God" (steps 8 through 12).

Forgiving does not mean that we excuse the action. Many people refuse to forgive certain actions because they see them as inexcusable. C. S. Lewis says, "To be a Christian means to forgive the inexcusable, because God has forgiven the inexcusable in you." Forgiving others is an important part of turning our will over to God. When we forgive others of the wrongs they have committed against us, we do not excuse what they have done. We simply recognize that we have been hurt unjustly and turn the matter over to God. Steps 8 and 9 are all about forgiving. These steps suggest that we must be ready and willing to make direct amends to all people that we have harmed.

In other words, we need to clean up our side of the street. We must repair the damage that we have caused. And we cannot do this unless we humble ourselves with a forgiving heart. Even if we feel that we were provoked or justified in the harm that we committed, we still must own up to our part. If we are resistant or hold on to resentments, the Big Book says that it will kill us. We must let go and come clean with a forgiving heart. Jesus says, "Therefore, if you are offering your gift at the altar and that your brother or sister has something against you, leave your gift there in front of the altar. First go and be reconciled to them; then come and offer your gift" (see Matthew 5:23–24). Scripture also says in 1 John 4:20, "Whoever claims to love God yet hates a brother and sister is a liar. For whoever does not love their brother or sister, whom they have seen, cannot love God, whom they have not seen." Therefore, we must be honest with ourselves and admit our part with a humble and forgiving heart and be reconciled with our fellows.

5. Love

The last but not the least essential element in our journey to the truth is "love." In fact, Apostle Paul claims in 1 Corinthians 13 that without love nothing else matters. Also, the final three steps (steps 10–12) of the AA recovery program say that we seek love and tolerance of others as our code. Step 12 suggests that having a spiritual awaking as the result of these steps, we carry the message of the new God-centered life to our fellows and practice these principles in all our affairs. Step 12 is all about being of service and helping our fellows with love find their way to freedom through faith in God. It is God's will that we love others. Love is more than a feeling; it is choosing to behave in a caring and loving way. With God's grace, His love grows in us as we place our trust in Him. We discover an inverse relationship between love and fear. Fear fades as our love grows. There are two basic emotions that drive our behavior; either fear or love. Ask anyone who loves their job, if they experience fear. In most cases, we discover that those who truly love what they do are filled with a passion that displaces any sense of fear. Usually those who hate their job will not seek out new opportunities for fear of failure, hence working as a slave in bondage out of fear.

The source of all love is from God. Apostle John wrote, "Dear friends, let us continue to love one another, for love comes from God. Anyone who loves is a child of God and knows God. But anyone who does not love does not know God, for God is love" (1 John 4:7–8). Jesus said, "I am giving you a new commandment: love each other. Just as I have loved you, you should love each other" (John 13:34). By God's grace, we receive His unconditional love and we begin to love ourselves. We are then told to love others as we love ourselves and as Jesus have loved us.

Scripture defines love this way, "Love is patient and kind. Love is not jealous or boastful or proud or rude. It does not demand its own way. It is not irritable, and it keeps no record of being wronged . . . Love never gives up, never loses faith, is always hopeful, and endures through every circumstance" (1 Corinthians 13:4–7). Finally, Apostle Paul says, "Three things will last forever—faith, hope, and love—and the greatest of these is love" (1 Corinthians 13:13). Without selfless love, we have nothing. Hence, the Bible tells us to "let love be your highest goal!" (1 Corinthians 14:1). By God's love for us and by His grace, we grow in love for Him and our fellows.

With this general outline of our new-found journey to the truth, we begin to see how the good news of the Gospel of Jesus Christ will transform our life from a life of bondage to a life of freedom in Christ. The old man is dead in sin and the new man is alive in Christ by grace. As apostle Paul states in 2 Corinthians 5:17, "Therefore, if anyone is in Christ, the new creation has come: The old has gone, the new is here!" See **Illustration 1** which depicts the transformed life by illustrating the dramatic change that takes place in one's life, attitude, nature and behaviors, values and beliefs, and purpose of life.

Illustration 1

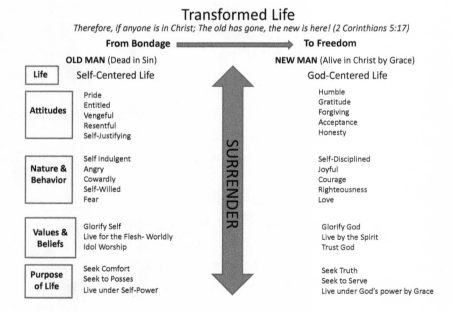

We are now ready to begin the arduous pilgrimage to freedom and truth. As we begin our journey, there are two essential building blocks that we must have firmly in place from the beginning. These building blocks consist of spirituality and fellowship. Both of these elements are foundational to our pathway to freedom. Since our problem is a spiritual malady, a firm understanding of the necessity of a spiritual awakening is paramount. And by this, we must not conflate spirituality with religion. Equally as important, is the realization of the difficulty of this journey.

Under no circumstance can this trip be taken alone without a competent guide and the help from our fellow travelers. With this in mind, I will turn in the next chapter to the all-important discussion regarding the good news of the Gospel and the promises of the twelve steps vs. religion followed by a chapter devoted to the imperative need for a loving fellowship. With these building blocks in place, we are then ready to embark on the step-by-step journey to freedom, truth and finally victory.

CHAPTER IV

Gospel-Inspired
Twelve-Step Program

1. Gospel and Twelve Steps vs. Religion

Alcoholics Anonymous maintains that it is not a religious organization. All members are free to decide their ideas about the meaning and purpose of life. However, the Twelve-Step Recovery Program also asserts that God's help through a spiritual awakening is necessary for recovery. Step 12 states, "Having had a spiritual awakening as the result of these steps . . ." This spiritual awakening is the purpose of the whole program. The Big Book stresses throughout the text the necessity of God's help as central to the recovery process. The Third Steps states that "we made a decision to turn our will and our lives over to the care of God." In fact, the essence of the whole program is that we cannot recover under our power, but "that God could and would if He were sought."

The program also encourages those who belong to religious denominations to seek their help and for those who are not members of religious bodies to be quick to see where religious people are right and "make use of what they offer." Also, like the

Bible, the AA program is a program of action. "We alcoholics are undisciplined. So we let God discipline us . . . But this is not all. There is action and more action. Faith without works is dead." This is taken nearly directly from the Book of James wherein James 2:26 states, "As the body without the spirit is dead, so faith without deeds is dead."

With any close reading of the Big Book, one will discover that there are few if any contradictions with the Bible. In fact, the AA founders and Bill W. himself have indicated that their recovery ideas came from the Bible, the Oxford Group, and the Reverend Sam Shoemaker from the Calvary Church in New York City. Also, Dr. Bob (AA's co-founder with Bill W.) as a member of the Oxford Group (a non-religious Christian Group) had excellent Bible training as a youngster. Even though Dr. Bob did not directly write the twelve steps, he spent countless hours with Bill W. late into many nights discussing the biblical concepts which were to be incorporated into the twelve steps. Most important, however, was the contribution from Rev. Sam Shoemaker. Bill W. acknowledged that it was through Rev. Sam Shoemaker that most of AA's spiritual principles have come. AA-derived much of its inspiration from Rev. Sam Shoemaker's Calvary Church in New York and Bill W attributes much of the development of the Twelve Steps to his teaching and writings.

While Alcoholics Anonymous claims that it is not a religious organization, but inspired by Christian writings and teachings; many Christian scholars also agree that Christianity is not a religion as well. Many Christian scholars consider Christianity to be a revelation of God versus a religion. In fact, Christianity is more often referred to as a faith. We often speak of "Christian faith." It is called a "faith" because the core of Christian belief is based on faith. R. C. Sproul claims that Christianity is a theology rather than a religion. Theology is the highest order of the science and study of the nature of God. It is a belief system with God at the center. The next order of study below theology is anthropology which is the science of humanity and religion is a sub-study of anthropology dealing with the behavior of man in its pursuit of a relationship with God. Consequently, theology is God-centered and religion is man-centered. R. C. Sproul also claims that religion which deals with the behavior of man's organization to worship God more often than not inadvertently tend to create idol worship.

Idol worship can be a problem for religion. The Bible warns against idol worship throughout both the Old Testament and the New Testament. The Book of Isaiah in the Old Testament talks about the people being blinded by looking into the face of idols. In fact, the first two commandments of the Ten Commandments forbid us from worshiping any other gods or bowing down to any idols. In the book *Christian Worldview* author Phillip Graham Ryken makes the point that everybody worships something. He quoted the author David Foster Wallace when he addressed Kenyon College with astonishing clarity about the centrality of worship (and its consequences):

> *"There is no such thing as not worshiping. Everybody worships. The only choice we get is what we worship. And the compelling reason for maybe choosing some sort of god or spiritual-type thing to worship . . . is that pretty much anything else you worship will eat you alive. If you worship money and things, if they are where you tap real meaning in life, then you will never have enough. Worship your body and beauty and sexual allure, and you always feel ugly. And when time and age start showing, you will*

die a million deaths before they finally grieve
you . . . Worship power, you will end up feeling
weak and afraid, and you will need even more
power over others to numb you to your own fear.
Worship your intellect, being seen as smart, you
will end up feeling stupid, a fraud, always on
the verge of being found out. But the insidious
thing about these forms of worship is . . . they're
unconscious. They are default settings."

In other words, what we worship matters and ultimately encompasses our entire perspective on the world. In fact, the Big Book emphasizes that the how and the why of the whole program is that: "First of all, we had to quit playing God. It didn't work. Next, we decided that hereafter in this drama of life, God was going to be our Director." For this reason, our worldview can never be reduced to a set of intellectual concepts. It is a matter of the heart as well as what we think and love. In the final analysis, the only life-saving worldview is one that leads to everlasting worship of God. Therefore, we discover that the Christian Gospel of Jesus Christ is a theology of God-centered faith. Likewise, the Twelve Steps of Alcoholics Anonymous is inspired and derived from the Gospel and incorporates the same core elements that are essential for both salvation and recovery.

The essence of this book is that the Gospel, not religion was revealed to me by the Twelve Steps of Alcoholics Anonymous. Since AA is not a religious organization, it is essential for anyone reading this book to recognize the fundamental difference between the gospel and religion. The principal difference is that religion is based on obeying a set of divine standards out of fear versus out of gratitude. The gospel depicts an attitude of gratitude for the gift of the blessings we have already received because of Christ. For our just God has already set the stage for our salvation. The game is over. It is finished. He won. There is nothing for us to do but to accept by faith His loving gift of Christ crucified. This gospel is indeed the good news. The moralist, however, is forced into obedience, motivated by fear of rejection. But the Christian rushes into obedience, driven by a desire to please and resemble the one who gave his life for us. Hence, the gospel provides true freedom. As stated in the Big Book, "True freedom is doing the right thing not because we ought to, but because we want to." Unfortunately only a fraction of Christian men has genuinely accepted the gift of the gospel. Hence, in most cases, their lives are not entirely shaped by the story of salvation. They have not wholly embraced the good news of the gospel. It is not just a matter of knowing it, but living it out each day. Generally speaking, the religious nature of the church too often misses the target by not fully grasping the Bible-based, Christ-centered, Spirit-empowered, God-glorifying perspective that belongs to us by grace—which is why we need to learn to live by the gospel verses religion.

Jesus also took a dim view of the religious and through the parable of the prodigal son, singles out religious moralist as a particularly deadly spiritual condition. Timothy Keller points out in his book *The Prodigal God* that Christianity was not considered a religion in its early days. Keller says, *"It was the non-religion. Imagine the neighbors of early Christians asking them about their faith. 'Where's your temple?' they'd ask. The Christians would reply that they didn't have a temple. 'But how could that be? Where do your priests labor?' The Christian would have replied that they didn't have priests. 'But . . . but,' the neighbors would have sputtered, 'where are the sacrifices made to please your gods?' The Christian would have responded that they did not make sacrifices anymore . . . Jesus himself was the temple to end all temples, the priest to end all priests, and the sacrifice to end all sacrifices."*

Timothy Keller claims that this was a foreign concept to the Romans; hence they referred to Christians as "atheists" because their belief system did not fit with any of the other religions of the world. Keller suggests further that the parable explains why they were right when insisting Christians were atheists. The point that Keller is making is that religious people, in general, were offended by Jesus and it was the non-religious that were attracted to him. This is born out throughout Gospel. Keller sights several verses (Luke 7, John 3–4, and Luke 19) where the outcast is the one who connects with Jesus, and the religious person does not. In Matthew 21:31, Jesus says to the religious leaders, "Truly I tell you, the tax collectors and the prostitutes are entering the Kingdom of God before you." Jesus's teaching consistently attracted the non-religious lost souls of his day. Jesus came to seek and to save those who were lost just like the prodigal son. Jesus says in Matthew 18:12 that He will "Go out and search for the one that is lost."

Ezekiel 34:11 says, "For this is what the sovereign Lord says: I myself will search and find my sheep. I will be like the shepherd looking for his scattered flock. I will find my sheep and rescue them from all the places where they were scattered on that dark and cloudy day."

In many cases, people don't begin to come to God until they stop being religious. The reason being is that there can be only one master. Only today do I recognize that the fundamental aspect of my transformation as described in "My Story" is that I don't need to prove myself anymore. I now have but one master—Almighty God. There is only one master of the human heart and soul which is Jesus Christ, not religion. And the Lord Jesus never insists for us to come to Him. He never says that you will come to me or submit to me. If our Lord insisted on our obedience, He would become merely a taskmaster. He never insists on obedience, but when we turn to Him and see Him, we will immediately obey Him.

The question now before us is whether the churches today have this same attraction that Jesus had in His day. It appears that too often the church draws legalistic, moralistic and often self-righteous people and does not provide a safe place for those who are lost. The broken and the lost in our society avoid church. Therefore, if the church is not attracting the lost, are their religious practices carrying the same message that Jesus had? The answer may lay in the emphasis on religion versus theology or faith. Whatever the case, Alcoholics Anonymous has taken the principles of Jesus teaching and incorporated them into their twelve-step program that has attracted the broken and lost due to alcoholism, drug abuse, sexual abuse or a host of many sinful obsessions.

2. Twelve Steps Derived from the Bible

The Eleventh Tradition of Alcoholics Anonymous speaks about the program of being one of attraction rather than promotion. The AA fellowship emphasizes sharing with the newcomer our story in a general way what we used to be like, what happened, and what we are like now. We never promote our way as a cure-all. We merely ask, as stated in the Big Book, "If you have decided you want what we have and are willing to go to any length to get it—then you are ready to take certain steps." This approach is derived directly from the gospel. Jesus never forces us to obey. But He is always available if we seek Him. In the parable of the prodigal son in Luke 15:31, the father says to the elder son, "Everything I have is yours." The father did not force the elder brother to partake in the feast. In fact, the elder brother was angry and refused to go in. Jesus says to follow Him. "But seek first . . . and all these things will be given to you . . ." (Matthew 6:33).

The essential difference between religion and the gospel is that the major religions of the world operate on the principle of obeying God to be accepted by God. The guiding principle of the gospel is that God accepts me through what Jesus Christ has done, and therefore I obey. Religion seeks self-salvation through good moral deeds. The gospel relies on faith in Christ crucified as our savior. The Twelve Steps also rely on God to rescue us from our wayward ways. In the first two steps, we admit that we are powerless and we come to believe in a power higher than ourselves to restore us to sanity. In other words, we must place all our trust in God to save us. This is what the third step means when it says, "Made a decision to turn our will and our lives over to the care of God." In AA, we don't try to do better. We let go and let God. We can't do it by ourselves; we need God's help. The Big Book describes a newfound power and presence as we let go and asked for His help. "He provided what we needed if we kept close to Him and performed His work well." The Big Book continues, "As we felt new power flow in . . . as we became conscious of His presence, we began to lose our fear of today, tomorrow or the hereafter. We were reborn." Here again, is the validation that the twelve-step principles are derived directly from the Gospel. The Big Book says, we must be "reborn" to recover, and the Bible says, we must be "born again" to enter the Kingdom of God.

While it has become clear that the twelve steps were derived from the gospel, it is also clear that there are several significant differences between the gospel and religion. As discussed earlier, religion relies on man-centered good deeds while the gospel relies on Jesus Christ as our savior. Secondly, there is a difference in motivation. In religion, we obey out of fear of receiving God's wrath. Whereas, in the gospel, the motivation is one of gratitude for the gift of grace received because of Christ. Another difference has to do with our identity or self-reliance. In religion, the reliance on good deeds often yields a sense of false pride or a feeling of "holier than thou" toward those off the path. The gospel develops a different identity. In Christ, we are accepted by grace despite our faults, and also, we are willing to admit them. In other words, I'm so flawed that Christ died for my sins and so loved that the Father gave His son for me. Hence, we are humbled but yet have a deep confidence at the same time. We are stripped of our false pride but yet feel we have nothing to prove to anyone anymore. For in the gospel, we have but one master who receives all the glory—almighty God. Religion tends to exclude, while the gospel is inclusive. A Christian's worth is never dependent on excluding anyone because "but for the grace of God, there go I."

Finally, religion and the gospel differ in the way they deal with the difficulties of trials and tribulations. In religion, there is a sense of being worthy because of the good moral life that is lead. Religious followers believe they deserve good happy life and if their life does not go well, anger, and resentments may develop. The gospel, on the other hand, does not claim high expectations of an excellent, deserving life. In fact, Jesus claims that if you follow Him, you should expect much difficulties and even persecution.

3. Twelve Steps and Spiritual Awakening

It is critical for anyone reading this book to understand the fundamental difference between the gospel and religion. I did not find God through religion but through the action plan of working the twelve-step recovery program. God revealed Himself to me as I worked and practiced the twelve-step program and received the gift of a spiritual awakening which led me to the gospel. In fact, step 12 states clearly, "Having had a spiritual awakening as the result of these steps . . ." Hence, the sole purpose of the twelve steps is to have a spiritual awakening. This is not an intellectual exercise. Scripture makes the same claim that the intellect only gets in the way. Apostle Paul says in 1 Corinthian 2:14, "But people who aren't spiritual can't receive these truths from God's Spirit. It all sounds foolish to them and they can't understand it, for only those who are spiritual can understand what the Spirit means."

Here, the Bible speaks about our spiritual blindness and our inability to recognize the need for God's help. What I received from working the twelve steps of Alcoholics Anonymous was a miraculous life-saving gift from a loving God. I gained a spiritual awakening as the result of the twelve steps that in turn revealed the Gospel of Jesus Christ by the grace of God.

Having discussed the difference between the Gospel and the 12-Steps vs. religion and the purpose of the 12-Steps is to have a spiritual awakening; it is of paramount importance to gain a basic understanding of the process of the 12-Step program before we begin our journey.

The most simplistic description of the 12-Step program is: (1) trust God, (2) clean house, and (3) help others. The Big Book expands on this by stating, "Abandon yourself to God as you understand God. Admit your faults to Him and to your fellows. Clear away the wreckage of your past. Give freely of what you find and join us." Let's unpack these statements in order:

1) Abandon yourself to God- -Steps 1-3. I can't, He can, let Him

    a. Step 1—We admitted we were powerless over alcohol—that our lives had become unmanageable.

    b. Step 2—Came to believe in a Power greater than ourselves could restore us to sanity.

    c. Step 3—Made a decision to turn our will and our lives over to the care of God *as we understand Him.*

2) Admit your faults to Him and to your fellows—Steps 4 and 5.

    a. Step 4—Made a searching and fearless moral inventory of ourselves.

    b. Step 5—Admitted to God, to ourselves and to another human being the exact nature of our wrongs.

3) Clear away the wreckage of the past—Steps 6-11.

    a. Step 6—Were entirely ready to have God remove all these defects of character.

    b. Step 7—Humbly ask Him to remove our shortcomings.

    c. Step 8—Made a list of all persons we had harmed, and became willing to make amends to them all.

    d. Step 9—Made direct amends to such people wherever possible, except when to do so would injure them or others.

    e. Step 10—Continued to take personal and when we were wrong promptly admitted it.

    f. Step 11—Sought through prayer and meditation to improve our conscious contact with God *as we understand Him,* praying only for knowledge of His will for us and the power to carry that out.

4) Give freely what you find and join us.

    a. Step 12—Having had a spiritual awakening as the result of these steps, we tried to carry this message to alcoholics, and to practice these principles in all our affairs.

The Big Book acknowledges that working these steps is a tall order. But the Program also concedes that alcohol is a powerful foe and without help, it is too much for us. The Big Book says, "But there is one who has all power—that one is God. May you find Him now! Half measures availed us nothing. We stood at the turning point. We asked His protection with complete abandon." The Steps constitute a rigorous action plan but the program admits that there is no expectation of perfect adherence to these principles. "We claim spiritual progress rather than spiritual perfection."

The twelve steps begin in Step-1 with the word "We" which suggest that we cannot take this journey on our own. It is also in this step that we admit we are powerless over alcohol. It is only in Step-1 that "alcohol" is even mentioned. This is where the word "alcohol" can be replaced with any other sinful obsession. Hence, the twelve step program is a design for living that provides an action plan not only for alcoholism, but for any sinful obsession that block us from seeking God's will. The twelve step program takes us on a God-centered path from total surrender and trusting God to having a spiritual awakening and a transformed life. See **Illustration 2** which depicts the Twelve-Step process action plan. The illustration takes us through the stages of open mindedness, faith, trust, honesty, repentance, willingness, humility, forgiveness, daily bread, prayer to a spiritual awakening and finally victory.

Illustration 2

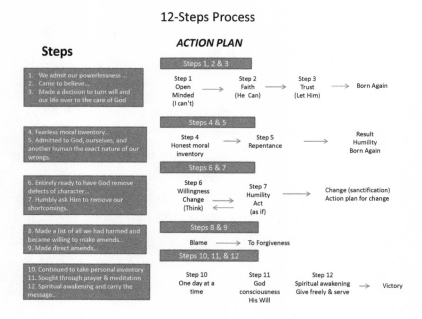

As we continue along our pathway to truth, let's now turn to another foundational building block of fellowship. As I stated earlier, we cannot take this journey alone, we need the help and support of our fellows—a loving fellowship.

CHAPTER V

Fellowship

The word "fellowship" is defined by *Merriam-Webster* as a relationship of people who share interests or feelings. It is further defined as a community of people who share interests, activity, feeling, or experience. Alcoholics Anonymous depicts their fellowship with a three-sided triangle representing: service, unity, and recovery. The fellowship is essential to recovery in that we support each other in our common problem in a unity of purpose. The AA Preamble begins as follows: "Alcoholics Anonymous is a fellowship of men and women who share their experience, strength and hope with each other that they may solve their common problem and help others to recover from alcoholism." The essence of the AA fellowship is that we cannot recover from this devastating spiritual malady on our own. We alone cannot transform ourselves. Even though we recognize it is God's power that changes our lives, we also appreciate the infusing power of the group that draws something more out of each of us than any of us by ourselves can supply. Hence, it is only by this unity of purpose that each of us, in turn, draws from the spiritual reservoir of the fellowships additional wisdom, strength and courage which makes each of us stronger and the fellowship more powerful.

The Gospel refers to the "Church" as a fellowship of those who believe in God, are reconciled to Him through Christ and made one in Christ. Thus, the Church is a fellowship of those who strive to live according to Jesus Christ's teaching and example of faith and love. Therefore, the outcome of faith and love should be unity. In the Gospel, Christ desires his disciples to be woven together in a single fellowship as harmonious as the unity of a healthy body. Apostle Paul describes this unity in 1 Corinthians 12:12–20, "Just as a body, though one, has many parts, but all its many parts form one body, so it is with Christ . . . As it is, there are many parts, but one body." Therefore, it is not uniformity but unity that is the essential part of the nature of fellowship in the church.

Jesus gathered around him a scattered group of men who followed him and were held together by an invisible bond of fellowship. Luke describes in Acts 2:42–47 the activities that characterized the early Christian community. "All the believers devoted themselves to the apostles' teaching, and to fellowship, and to sharing in meals, and to prayer. A deep sense of awe came over them all . . . And all the believers met together in one place and shared everything they had . . . They worshiped together at the temple each day, met in homes for the Lord's Supper . . . And each day the Lord added to their fellowship those who were being saved." Their faith, joy, and loving support were contagious and many more became believers. The AA recovery fellowship follows much of the same pattern as we grow in faith, for it is never done in isolation. We need the help of others to walk with us daily, encouraging us when we become discouraged and holding us accountable when we stray.

The early Church provides us a standard of what true fellowship is and its importance in developing and growing in a spiritual relationship with God. However, the fellowship activities of the church today seem to be a world apart from the early church. The fact that the church today provides a venue to share social events with other Christians does not of itself imply fellowship. C. S. Lewis described the purpose of the Church very simply: "The Church exists for nothing else but to draw men into Christ, to make them little Christ's. If they are not doing that, all the cathedrals, clergy, missions, sermons, even the Bible itself, are simply a waste of time. God became Man for no other purpose. It is even doubtful, you know, whether the whole universe was created for any other purpose." On the other hand, the AA fellowship appears to make good use of principles of fellowship practiced by the early church. They do profess a singleness of purpose to carry the message to the alcoholic that still suffers. The fellowship of Alcoholics Anonymous must survive in the fulfillment of its true purpose for it is often a matter of life and death.

As the Big Book says, "Therefore, no society of men and women ever had a more urgent need for continuous effectiveness and permanent unity. We alcoholics see that we must work together and hang together, else most of us will finally die alone." Even though we all suffer the same spiritual malady of our sinful nature, the AA fellowship takes to heart the life and death consequences of its predicament. Too often the Christian fellowship takes their society to lightly when they equate various social activities with a true fellowship with the purpose of bringing men to Christ. The organized Church is desperately ill-suited to promote the necessary unity and singleness of purpose if its members do not see themselves possessing a spiritual malady and in need of recovery at a level of spiritual life and death. All too often members exhibit a spiritual pride, prejudice, and narrow-mindedness.

The Christian fellowship has four essential elements. First, it is two-dimensional consisting of first a vertical plane and then a horizontal plane of fellowship. Second, it is a two-way street where its members help each other. Third, it is an expression of both love and humility, and finally, it is a gift of God by His grace. The first truth to consider about Christian fellowship is that it is not an end in itself. Fellowship between Christians (horizontal plane) is for the sake of fellowship with God (vertical plane). Fellowship with God (vertical plane) is the purpose of all fellowship and without it; the essence of Christianity is lost.

Fellowship with God is, therefore, the source from which fellowship among Christians emanates. But it is also true, that our society with fellow Christians is essential in feeding our fellowship with God. Our fellowship with God stems from our recognition of what God has done for us. When God blesses us with His grace, we receive a sense of gratitude for the gift of salvation that God provided through His Son. When we take the Lord Jesus Christ as our Savior, we become children of God the Father. Jesus said, "He who receives me, receives Him who sent me" (Matthew 10:40). Filled with the Holy Spirit and a heart full of gratitude, we seek to please the Father through daily revelations of Himself from His Word. We worship God through prayer and obedience which forms the bases of our fellowship with Him. The Holy Spirit helps us to fellowship with God, but we are also directed to share with our fellows to increase our spiritual growth in Christ. By sharing with fellow Christians our revelations of God, we both gain in our knowledge of God and enrich our fellowship with Him.

Secondly, the fellowship is a two-way street. As we share our experience, strength, and hope in Christ with our fellows; not only do we give, but we also gain in spiritual growth. One of the spiritual paradoxes that we express in the AA fellowship is that: "We must give it away to keep it." In other words, as we share our experience, strength and hope to help and encourage others, we gain strength and courage ourselves. Apostle Paul describes this well in Romans 1:11–12, "I long to see you so that I may impart to you some spiritual gift to make you strong— that is, that you and I may be mutually encouraged by each other's faith." The fellowship that Paul describes is apparently a two-way street. Paul acknowledges that he needs fellowship not only for him to help and encourage, but for his encouragement as well. Put another way; the teacher learns when teaching the student, while the student is preparing the teacher. The AA fellowship embraces this concept fully as sponsors gain spiritual growth while guiding the newcomer through the twelve steps to help them to achieve a spiritual awakening.

This concept of a two-way street of helping to be helped provides the foundation of the third essential element in Christian fellowship as an expression of both love and humility. The principle idea of AA fellowship meetings is to provide a safe place for those struggling with despair to find comfort, support, hope, and direction. The AA fellowship claims that "love and tolerance for others is our code." The fellowship also breeds an atmosphere of humility by constantly suggesting, "But for the grace of God, there go I." A true fellowship is a group where humility is foundational, and with God's presence, love and grace prevail.

Finally, a fellowship is indeed a gift from a loving God by His grace. When the Holy Spirit invades our hearts and souls, we desire a place to share our experience, strength and hope to help anyone who wants it. Through fellowship, one's heart and soul is nourished and refreshed. We are uplifted and inspired by sharing what God has done for us, and as we give this away to help others, we gain strength and spiritual wisdom. This is God's plan and is all provided by His grace.

All Christians need fellowship just as the AA fellowship is the lifeblood of the recovering alcoholic. None of us are spirituality self-sufficient. In fact, the single most significant obstacle to true fellowship is an attitude of spiritual self-sufficiency. There can be no fellowship where a view of autonomy prevails or a group think that they got it together and are only there to help and they are not in need of help. There are many other obstacles to true fellowship, such as, formality, elitism and any development of cliques. But there is none greater than the self-sufficient Christian.

One of Jesus's most important teaching to his disciples about humility and a mind-set of service is when Jesus began the washing of their feet as described in John 13:4–5. This was a great lesson in fellowship, humility, and service. In this case, Jesus teaches by example. The disciples may have been somewhat confused or even shocked when Jesus began washing the disciples' feet one by one. Jesus even stated in John 13:7, "You do not realize now what I am doing, but later you will understand." The reason the disciples must have been confused is that foot-washing, though necessary in those days, was always relegated to the lowly servants. Jesus did not come as a proud master demanding service but as a humble servant seeking to help others. Jesus preached what he was practicing: "Now that I, your Lord and Teacher, have washed your feet, you also should wash one another's feet. I have set you an example that you should do as I have done for you . . . Now that you know these things, you will be blessed if you do them" (John 13:14–16). The essence of Jesus teaching is humility and taking on a servant's role is the best evidence of humble life. This teaching came after the disciples were arguing about their importance. Jesus had previously explained that "many who are first will be last, and last first" (Mark 10:31). Placing ourselves in the position of servant humbles us and brings us closer to being Christlike. As we follow the example of Jesus, we look for opportunities to serve others. In AA, we help our fellows by sharing our story, listening to their difficulties, feeling their pain and supporting them through tough times. As we serve others and aid them in their recovery, we are strengthened in our recovery.

Christians today are lacking in fellowship. The church's so-called fellowship meetings may be friendly gatherings to get better acquainted or provide some needed service or help in some mission effort, but they severely lack in the real purpose of fellowship as helping each other to draw closer to Christ. I have attended both small group bible study meetings as well as the broader Bible Study Fellowship (BSF) meetings and to varying degrees; they both lack the real purpose of helping each other through love and humility to bring each other into a stronger relationship with Christ. The AA fellowship, on the other hand, has a singleness of purpose to help each other to find a solution to our common problems through humility by surrendering to God on a daily bases. Everyone in the AA fellowship is in dire need of support of their fellows. There is no status or privilege to be gained for everyone is seen at the same level in this society. All members are considered just one drink away from fatal disaster. Therefore, out of necessity members must adhere to the program (without rules or requirements) or they may perish. AA members must stick together lest they die. Hence, the AA adage, "Love and tolerance for others is our code."

The AA fellowship adheres to most of the Christian principles for real fellowship, and the church would do well to take notice of what AA has to offer. The most important thing that the church can gain from AA is that there must be a defined need that all members are desperately seeking to change their ways. In other words, you won't get anywhere unless you know where you want to go. People understand why they come to AA. They may not at first want to come, but they know that they are not there to get just a little better. They are not there because it sounds like a good idea. In fact, in my case, it was the last place on earth where I want to be. People come to AA because they are desperate. They are not looking for religion; in fact, to the contrary, they are desperately lost in search of redemption. The twelve-by-twelve describes it well, "Under the lash of alcoholism we are driven to AA, and there we discover the fatal nature of our situation. Then, and only then, do we become as open-minded to conviction and as willing to listen as the dying can be. We stand ready to do anything which will lift this merciless obsession from us." Without the AA fellowship, death is staring us in the face. AA is the last house on the block. If this doesn't explicitly define a need, I don't know what will. What AA provides is a new life and the much-needed hope to receive it. AA delivers a solution and the pathway to get there with the help of God and the fellowship. And this solution does not consist of changing our ways, but a total transformation from a self-centered life to a God-centered life. And there are not many ways, or a couple of ways, there is one way; we either find it or perish.

Now compare this with those joining a Christian fellowship. Most Christians joining a fellowship already consider themselves pretty good Christians (if there is such a thing). If not, they certainly don't consider themselves desperate by any means. They are usually looking for a better understanding of the Bible, or they would like to become a better Christian. These are undoubtedly worthy desires, but they do not even begin to compare to the defining need of the alcoholic. The irony is that the Gospel says that we are dead in our transgressions. We are all sinners, and without salvation, we are dead. So like the alcoholic, we all suffer from a fatal nature of our situation. The question is, does the Christian fellowship recognize the seriousness of the spiritual malady and define clearly what our needs are.

All too often, the Christian fellowship falls into a mindset of becoming too performance oriented. Members tend to clothe themselves with the pretense of looking good for Jesus. We tend to put on our so called respectable Christian mask in an effort to look like a good representative of Jesus. Hence, the fellowship becomes a performance competition of looking good on the outside vs. breaking down our façade and coming clean in honest testimony by sharing the mess on our insides. Since we are supposed to look good to our brothers in Christ, the church becomes an uncomfortable environment for those of us who are not in a place where we can pretend that we have our life together. Therefore, we shy away from the support we need and simply don't go. Unfortunately, the church and its Christian fellowship can become an unwelcome place for those most in need.

The biggest thing that turns people away from church is the perception of hypocrisy. The fact is that none of us are that good. We are all sinners and in need of help from Christ's sufficiency and from our brothers in Christ. Consider the difference if the church dropped the idea of its members being spiritually strong vs. being spiritually broken or in need of spiritual help to grow in Christ. Instead of feeling embarrassed about seeking help and prayer, we can feel the comfort and freedom of all of us being in the same boat. The idea that we are all in the same boat is the essence of the AA fellowship. In AA, no one is better than anyone else. We have all walked in the same shoes and are either climbing or have climbed out of the same dark hole.

Another critical factor is that AA is seeking to redeem members with a total transformation in a life-changing fellowship. The fellowship aims for a complete transformation from a self-centered life to a God-centered life. The concept of AA is not to change this or that in order get better. The idea is to change everything to develop a whole new attitude and outlook on life. A life-changing fellowship is what the original Church was all about. Few churches today replicate this model while the survival of the AA fellowship is entirely dependent upon the thorough application of the life-changing model of the early Church. In AA, our relationship with God only grows as we help others develop a God-centered life. The fellowship that redeems us will wither and die if we don't continually give what has been freely given to us. Again, we must give it away to keep it. This statement represents a core principle of the recovery. Also, humility is the spiritual foundation of all of the twelve steps of the AA recovery program.

AA also incorporates the idea that we feel your pain because we have been there. Nobody knows what it is like to be an alcoholic if you are not one. The fellowship is all about one drunk helping another drunk. If you haven't walked in my shoes, then you have no business talking to me. In AA, we can get down at the same level of those who are dying of this fatal malady because we have been there. We don't speak from above, lecture or preach. We share our experience, strength, and hope. We tell our story to gain the suffering alcoholic's confidence. Also, we are not fooled by their excuses, rationalization, and self-justification. In other words, we don't buy into their pack of lies. We don't give pats on the back for trying harder. You are either all in, or you're not. The Big Book says, "Half measures availed us nothing. We stood at the turning point. We asked His protection and care with complete abandon." Recovery is a matter of life and death. We are dealing with desperate people in desperate situations, and drastic measures must be taken.

Finally, the AA fellowship provides an environment in which the members feel confident that they are in a safe place where they can share their most dire vulnerabilities. The society offers an atmosphere where one can expose their weaknesses by shedding their many layers of self-justification. In other words, quit the lie and get honest with oneself and tell on ourselves. We take off the layers of clothes that shield us from our true nature—the facade that we hide behind in fear of exposing ourselves. In fact, the ability to get honest with ourselves is the essential requirement for recovery. On the other hand, the Christian fellowship often establishes an environment that achieves the exact opposite. As discussed above, there is the tendency to add clothes such as additional robes that provides the pretense of piety to cover up any sinful nature. Therefore, the church fellowship drapes itself in the goodness of its members. In essence, the members seek to show their goodness versus reveal their weakness and sinful nature. This is contrary to the core truth of the depravity of man. Without this recognition, there is no room for the solution.

God wants us to fellowship. We were not born to develop a spiritual life on our own, or to search for God by seeking a serene spiritual retreat. We are born for a great purpose in life which is to develop a full realization of Jesus Christ, which in turn pursues the building of His body. With this goal in mind, the question becomes; am I building up the body of Christ, or am I only concerned with my personal spiritual development? Far too often we get caught up in self-realization vs. God-realization. Self-realization only leads to the glorification of good works, whereas a saint of God glorifies Jesus Christ through his good works. Godly men glorify God, and Godless men glorify self.

CHAPTER VI

Abandon Yourself to God
(*Steps 1-3*)

The Gospel of Jesus Christ and the Promises of the AA Big Book
Born Again and We were Reborn
Surrender, Surrender, Surrender
I can't, God could, Let God

The most well-known adage when purchasing real estate is "Location, location, and location." Well, there is a similar adage in seeking spiritual truth, which is, "Surrender, surrender, and surrender." As we discussed in chapter 3 ("Pathway to Truth"), the search for spiritual truth begins with "surrender" and each essential element we encounter along the pathway demands a continual surrender, or if you will, an act of humility. Surrender and humility are two words that are often used interchangeably in describing spiritual development. To surrender means to yield to power or to give oneself up to power as in abandon oneself. Humility means appreciating our proper role in God's world. In other words, when we talk about surrender, we humble ourselves to our God, or we submit to a power greater than ourselves. We abandon ourselves to God. The Gospel is clear in that we cannot obtain salvation by our efforts and the Twelve Steps also suggests "that probably no human power could have relieved our alcoholism and that God could and would if He were sought." This chapter begins the working journey to a New Life with the first three steps of Alcoholics Anonymous. In simple terms, the first three steps can be explained as *I can't, God could, Let God.* We begin with step 1 with the support of the truth of The Gospel.

1. I Can't

Step 1: *We admitted we were powerless over alcohol (sin)—that our lives had become unmanageable.*

    Job 6:11–13: *"But I don't have the strength to endure . . . No, I am utterly helpless, without any chance of success."*

    Romans 3:10–12: *"There is no one righteous, not even one; there is no one who understands; there is no one who seeks God. All have turned away; they have together become worthless; there is no one who does good, not even one."*

We begin our journey by admitting that we are power-less and therefore our life is unmanageable with little hope of success. The Big Book begins the process by taking directly from scripture that we are helpless unless we first admit the predicament in which we find ourselves. We must give up the denial of our problems and the idea that we are not that bad. One cannot solve a problem unless one admits to the challenge and can honestly identify what the problem is. Scripture states that man's core problem is a state of sin that is universal. The

Bible speaks of sin as an offense against God. Sin is described as turning away from God and relying on our resources as if we are separate from God and therefore self-reliant. Hence, scripture says that we are living not for God, but for ourselves. The Big Book states that we are selfish and self-centered. "That, we think, is the root of our troubles." Like the lepers in the Bible, the problem of the alcoholic is easily identifiable. Both were rebuked by society. But alcoholism is just a symptom of the cause being selfish pride. Therefore, the core problem is universal to all man which is a spiritual malady.

It is natural and inevitable for every man to sin. Scripture says, "There is no one righteous, not even one . . . there is no one who seeks God . . . . all have turned away . . . no one does good, not even one . . . for all have sinned and fall short of the glory of God" (Romans 3:10–12, 23). Therefore, the core of the problem for the alcoholic is the same problem for all man which is sin, and the great sin is self-centered pride. So the Big Book states, "Our troubles are of our own making, which arise out of ourselves and the alcoholic is an extreme example of self-will run riot, though he usually doesn't think so." Therefore, the primary obstacle to the solution is our human nature to self-justify. Our sinful nature causes us to deny our wayward ways. The Big Book states that we are driven by, "Fear, self-delusion, self-seeking and self-pity." Therefore, the first step in recovery and our salvation is to admit our powerlessness. To accept our powerlessness, unmanageability, utter defeat, and hopelessness is a requirement to begin the recovery process. We must surrender to the process.

Jesus Christ in the Sermon on the Mount said, "Blessed are the poor in spirit . . . Blessed are the meek, for they will inherit the earth" (Matthew 5:3–5). We cannot experience reconciliation with God without true humility. Pride is the number one obstacle which stands in the way of our dealing with painful problems and our destructive curse. When we cannot admit our sins, there is no cure. But when we humble ourselves to our God and surrender in total defeat, the pain begins to heal, and we receive the comfort that only God can provide. Job, of the Bible, also suffered such overwhelming pain that he wished he could die. But Job turned to petition God for he recognized that God was the only one who could take away the pain. The Big Book also provides God with the only answer to our self-inflicted pain and suffering from our sinful ways. The Big Book says, "Many of us had moral and philosophical convictions galore, but we could not live up to them even though we would have liked to. Neither could we reduce our self-centeredness much by wishing or trying on our own power. We had to have God's help." We now turn to step 2.

2. He Could

Step 2: *Came to believe that a power greater than ourselves could restore us to sanity.*

Hebrews 11:1: *"Faith is the confidence that what we hope for will actually happen; it gives us assurances about things we cannot see."*

Luke 15:20: *"But while he was still a long way off, his father saw him and was filled with compassion for him; he ran to his son, threw his arms around him and kissed him."*

Step 2 is considered the "hope" step. In step 2, our situation is assuredly not hopeless. The AA fellowship is where hope is born. Hope is the central theme of both The Gospel and the twelve-step program. When we finally come to an acceptance of our predicament, there is a sense of hopelessness, despair, and indeed a level of discouragement. Hope, however, is the key that unlocks the door of discouragement. The AA program promises that there is a solution if I look to God or a power greater than myself, I will always have hope. Having come to understand the spiritual axiom that I keep what I share, every time I encourage, I receive courage. Step 2 helps us to guard against discouragement when we set unrealistic expectations— from wanting to change the world by the weekend. Despair is a warning signal that we may have wandered across the God line.

Step 2 is also considered the "faith" step. When we come to believe, we begin to cross the bridge of reason to the desired shore of faith. The Bible claims that faith can make even the impossible happen—even move mountains. In Hebrews 11:1, "Faith is the confidence that what we hope for will actually happen; it gives us assurances about things we cannot see." Also, Hebrews 11 has been called the "Hall of Faith." It mentions a long list of Old Testament characters that were used by God because of their faith. Jesus said, "Everything is possible for one who believes" (Mark 9:23). Hebrews 11:6 states, "Anyone who wants to come to him must believe that God exists and that he rewards those who sincerely seek him." The Big Book in chapter 4, "We Agnostics" provides the question that we must ask if we are going to believe: "When we became alcoholics, crushed by a self-imposed crisis we could not postpone or evade, we had to fearlessly face the proposition that either God is everything or else He is nothing. God either is, or He isn't. What was our choice to be?" The Bible says in 1 Corinthians 15:17, "And if Christ has not been raised, then your faith is useless and you are still guilty of your sins."

In essence, Paul is saying that God either is all powerful or He isn't. If God could raise Jesus from the dead, then He has the power to do anything! If, however, God did not raise Jesus from the dead, then God is powerless, and we are lost. But apostle Paul provides us with everlasting hope by affirming the truth that Jesus did rise from the dead giving us all access to the greatest power in the universe—God himself. The Big Book goes on to describes how our sense of reason can only take us so far. It explains the difficulty of stepping from the solid footing of the bridge of Reason to the shore of Faith. But at last, we step from the bridge to shore. The Big Book says, "For the first time, he lived in conscious companionship with his Creator."

Finally, step 2 is played out in Jesus parable of the "Prodigal Son" where the father's great compassion for his returning son portrays God's love for those who are lost. This parable captures the nature of God's love for us in redeeming lost souls. The parable typifies the story of the alcoholic that must hit bottom in utter despair before he is able to ask for help. Like so many of us who identify with the younger son who left his father taking his share of the father's estate and venture out on his own to a far country where he squandered his wealth in wild living.

After losing everything and nearly starving to death, he came to his senses and returned to his father with shame and guilt. This story depicts our human nature of turning away from our father with our desire to be self-reliant and living life on our terms. For many of us it takes a state of absolute desperation for us to recognize our way doesn't work. So he returned home to his father. The parable says, "But while he was still a long way off, his father saw him and was filled with compassion for him; he ran to his son, threw his arms around him and kissed him" (Luke 15:20). This parable shows that no matter how washed-up or insane our life may become, there is always hope for a better way of life.

Like the father in this story, God waits for the sinner to return to Him on his own volition, but our heavenly Father does not wait for total amends or for us to completely clean up our act before embracing us with His love. "For this son of mine was dead and is alive again; he was lost and is found. So they began to celebrate." This story demonstrates that there is always hope when we stray from the path. All we need to do is turn back or look to our loving Father who actively seeks those of us who have strayed like lost sheep. We now turn to step 3 where we make the decision of our life.

3. Let Him

Step 3: *Made a decision to turn our will and our lives over to the care of God as we understand Him.*

Deuteronomy 30:15–20: *"Now listen! Today I am giving you a choice between life and death, between prosperity and disaster . . . you can make this choice by loving the Lord your God, obeying him, and committing yourself firmly to Him. This is the key to your life."*

John 3:3–7: *"I tell you the truth, unless you are born again, you cannot see the Kingdom of God . . . I assure you, no one can enter the Kingdom of God without being born of water and spirit . . . you must be born again."*

Proverbs 14:12: *"There is a path before each person that seems right, but it ends in death."*

Matthew 11:28–30: *"Come to me, all of you who are weary and carry heavy burdens, and I will give you rest . . . For my yoke is easy to bear, and the burden I give you is light."*

James 4:4–7: *"So humble yourself before God. Resist the devil, and he will flee from you. Come close to God, and God will come close to you."*

This is the turning point. We can no longer avoid our situation or evade our responsibility. This is "The Great Decision"—life or death. Everyone has this life or death decision to make. We have all been created with a free will—the ability to choose. The freedom of choice brings with it the burden of the consequences of our choices. Free will is both our blessing and our responsibility. God gave Moses a choice between life and death, between prosperity and disaster. Today, we all have two choices or a decision between two paths to follow:

    a)   God-centered life: Life
    b)   Self-centered life: Death

Scripture claims that we all inherited from Adam the nature of a self-centered life. The Big Book claims that selfishness and self-centeredness is the root our troubles driven by fear, self-delusion, self-seeking, and self-pity. We must surrender or abandon ourselves to God to receive the gift of God's grace. "But if your heart turns away and you refuse to listen . . . you will certainly be destroyed" (Deuteronomy 30:17–18), "You can make this choice by loving the Lord your God, obeying him, and committing yourself firmly to him. This is the key to your life." We must make this life-saving decision.

The third step states that "We made a decision to turn our lives and our will over to the care of God . . ." This is the most important decision of a lifetime or if you will—the great surrender. In the first two steps, we accepted our problem and began to believe that we need God's help, but now we must not only lay down the sword but let it go completely by placing all our trust in God. We must let go of our old ways of thinking, our false pride, self-reliance, and the need to always be right. This thinking must go! We let go of all our old ideas and admit we were wrong and abandon ourselves to God. This decision for life vs. death seems like a no-brainer. Like Bill W. said in his story, "Simple, but not easy; a price had to be paid." In fact, it is near impossible without God's help. The winds are blowing against us. We must set a new course or die. The storms of life are gathering power. We can no longer fight. We must yield and set a new course. We can't change the wind we are powerless. We need to adjust our sails and take on a new tact—a new course, go with the flow, yield, let go of the fight and set a new course and surrender to victory.

An unknown author stated it as follows: "One boat goes east, one boat goes west, by the self-same winds that blow. It's the set of the sails and not the gales that determine which way they go." In other words, no matter how dire our situation, God has given us a choice and it is our responsibility to act. God waits for us to come to Him on our own volition. But once we act. Once we make the decision to commit our lives to God, He comes running to our aid, as the father did in the Prodigal Son. We cross the bridge of Reason to the shores of Faith to a new life—a life with the risen Son.

The Bible claims that it is not by our action, but because of our action that we are reconciled to God and receive His redemptive power. Hence, we must take the initiative, but it is

He who does the work by His grace alone. Therefore, "Come to Me . . ." (Matthew 11:28). The word *come* means "to act." And the only action that God asks from us is to make a choice. This should not be so difficult. We either decide to come to Him as in the Prodigal Son, or we continue to turn away. For some strange prideful reason, the last thing we want to do is come. But everyone who does make this decision to come knows that this is the turning point, when God invades our life. When God invades our life, He breaks the hard outer shell of our independence from Him. We become liberated from the bondage of self, and our nature becomes aligned with God.

This breaking of my hard outer shell is explained in chapter 1 of "My Story" when my wife lovingly described how I had let her down along with my whole family. At first, I tried to mentally (not verbally) defend myself by self-justification and minimizing my behavior. As my mind was racing to push back, I was suddenly struck by a piercing pain resulting from the realization that she was right and I had no justification. This penetrating pain obviously had broken my hard outer layer of obstinacy toward God. I related this to being struck by God like Saul on the road to Damascus. God was asking me why I was persecuting Him. As explained in "My Story," whenever we are defiant, self-willed and set in our own ways, we are hurting God. This was my turning point.

Step 3 is often called the keystone step. The keystone represents the stone at the peak of an arch which holds the triumphant arch in place as we pass through to freedom. The Big Book begins the third step by claiming that first of all we had to quit playing God for it didn't work. The step ends by proclaiming that we were reborn while scripture says that we must be born again to enter the Kingdom of God. Spiritual rebirth is as necessary to the recovery process as it is to enter the Kingdom of God. This step of being born again is only the beginning or a baby step in the process. The hard part comes day in and day out as we submit our stubborn heart and will to the control of God's spirit. "Jesus replied, I assure you, no one can enter the Kingdom of God without being born of water and the Spirit" (John 3:5).

The AA program suggests that the effectiveness of the whole program rests on how earnestly we commit to the decision to align our will with God's will. This is not easy, in fact, close to impossible. But having reached a state of desperation, we become willing and the more willing we come to depend on God, the spirit of God comes to the rescue. Also, any effort to know God's will is aided by being open to it. The more we are open to learning God's will for us, the more likely God will reveal Himself to us. We usually know what we want, but often our wants are not the best for us. As we open ourselves up to God, we begin to recognize that He always provides for our needs but not necessarily our wants. God knows what is best for us, for only He knows the future. We may think that what we want is good for us.

But the good is the enemy of the best. When we decide to turn to God willingly, He does not only come to our aid, but He comes running to us with open arms with His love and grace. As described in the parable of the Prodigal Son, "For this son of mine was dead and is alive again; he was lost and is found. So they began to celebrate" (Luke 15:24).

We discover that willingness is the key to opening the door in step 3, but self-will often slams the door shut. This is a program of action, and step 3 is the beginning of the action steps. Making a decision is an action, for it commits us to a new direction. We are responsible for the action and what we turn over are the results, which we trust God to provide. So what precisely is the action to be taken? We only need to make a decision that we are committed to being open to God's way. In other words, surrender to the process and leave the results up to God. We don't just *believe* in God, but we *believe* God. In other words, we place all our trust in Him. When we do this, we begin to receive God's help in doing for us what we could not do for ourselves. Trusting God is the beginning of the miracle.

Again, in "My Story" I explain how this step-three was my first real struggle in the program. The idea that I was to give up control of my life was unthinkable for a self-willed control freak like me. I took great pride in my self-reliance and considered this to be a great virtue. Hence, it seemed absurd to consider this virtue as the cause of my problem. It took my sponsor to explain that all I had to do is make a decision. Realizing that I had been able to make decisions throughout my career, this should not be so difficult. However, this was like no other decision. This was a choice of life or death. Therefore, it should be a no-brainer . . . choose life. Yes, but choosing God's way means giving up my old life. This was not easy for me and is not easy for most. A choice has to be made, and a price has to be paid. As Bill W. said in "Bill's Story," "It meant the destruction of self-centeredness."

As I stated in "My Story," in looking back, this was truly the greatest decision of my life. The choice of either continuing down the road of the self-centered life or turning to this new path of a God-centered life had to be made. It was that simple; either I'm all in, or I'm not, what was my choice to be. I made the ultimate commitment; I'm all in! I chose God, and again everything then changed. Suddenly, the idea of giving up control to God didn't seem so difficult. I didn't realize it at the time, what I see today; that God was doing for me what I could not do for myself.

We are at the turning point. We have been on the wrong path all along. As Proverbs 14:12 states, "There is a path before each person that seems right, but it ends in death." Scripture explains that our sinful nature is inherited from Adam and that we are all on the path of destruction and in need of salvation. The Big Book describes our desperate need to change our ways. We must choose a new path. The program suggests that we must put all our chips on the line. We must be all in. The Big Book says, "Half measures availed us nothing. We stood at the turning point. We asked His protection and care with complete abandon." This new path is the God-centered path vs. the Self-centered way that we've been pursuing our whole life.

How then do we get off this path of destruction and on to this new God-centered way of life? Both scripture and the twelve-step program claim that God does the work, but they both maintain that we must begin the process by taking action. In all cases, the action starts with the decision and the time to begin is now. There is nothing to get ready for when we are desperate, even though the Big Book suggests that we be ready. We simply decide to put all our chips on God. The Big Book emphasizes the great importance of this decision by stating, "We thought well before taking this step making sure we were ready; that we could at last abandon ourselves utterly to Him . . . This was only the beginning, though if honestly and humbly made, an effect, sometimes a very great one, was felt at once. Next, we launched out on a course of vigorous action."

Scripture describes the action and the effect in several different ways. In Matthew 12:28–30 Jesus says, "Come to me, all of you who are weary and carry heavy burdens, and I will give you rest . . . For my yoke is easy to bear, and the burden I give you is light." In other words, Jesus is saying that He will give us comfort and relieve us of our burdens, if we will just abandon our ways and come to Him. It may seem difficult, but once we take this simple action and come to Him, it will be easy. James puts it another way in James 4:4–8, "So humble yourself before God. Resist the devil, and he will flee from you. Come close to God, and God will come close to you."

In conclusion, our part is quite simple: we make a decision that we are all in, we get honest with ourselves, humble ourselves, and most important, come to God. We have been putting off this decision our whole life. But when we are lost and in total despair, out of desperation, we thank God that He has given us the free will to choose Him, the gift of life. Thank God for His love. This brings us to steps 4 and 5 where we come clean and admit our wrongs to ourselves, God and another human being.

CHAPTER VII

Coming Clean--Repentance

Admit your faults to Him and your fellows (Steps 4 and 5)

Steps 4 and 5 is the point where real humility and honesty with one's self must prevail. This is the point in our journey where we come face to face with ourselves. We no longer run from the truth. For the first time in our lives, we face up to the truth about ourselves and come clean. The truth is that our self-deception and self-justification must cease to win over our thinking. We are asked to face the truth of our sinful ways and confess our sins to God and another human being.

We begin this process with a vigorous action of personal housecleaning which most of us had never attempted. After making the great decision to make the ultimate surrender in step 3, the Big Book suggests that "it could have little permanent effect unless at once followed by a strenuous effort to face, and be rid of, the things in ourselves which had been blocking us." It is only with God's help are we able to muster up the honesty and humility to come clean and confess our sins. This is not easy, but we must repent. Every one of us.

Step 4: *Made a searching and fearless moral inventory of ourselves.*

Matthew 7:5: *"You Hypocrites, first take the plank out of your own eye, and then you will see clearly to remove the speck from your brother's eye."*

Isaiah 53:6: *"We all, like sheep, have gone astray, each of us has turned to our own way . . ."*

Romans 3:10–12: *"There is no one righteous, not even one; there is no one who understands; there is no one who seeks God. All have turned away; they have together become worthless; there is no one who does good, not even one."*

Isaiah 6:5: *"Woe is me, for I am lost, for I am a man of unclean lips."*

Before we can fix anything, we must recognize where it is broken. This is often the most critical and challenging part of the process of making things run right again. It may be the most difficult, but it is always the most critical. If the diagnosis is not correct, the remedy will not solve the problem. With a missed diagnosis, the treatment more often than not treats the symptom rather than the core problem.

Proper diagnostics is critical whether it is your auto mechanic or your physician treating a medical ailment. But when addressing the human condition for a spiritual malady, it is next to impossible to recognize our failings. We are always ready to blame or criticize others versus looking at ourselves. Most of us are very quick to say, "I'm not that bad" or "look at those people" or "yeah but." As I explained in "My Story," I was a master at self-deception and self-justification. We are blind to our own brokenness. We have ears, but cannot hear; we have eyes, but cannot see.

As Matthew suggests in his gospel, we are too busy trying to fix others that we don't recognize our own brokenness. In Matthew 7:5 he states, "You hypocrites, first take the plank out of your own eye, and then you will see clearly to remove the speck from your brother's eye." Because of our pride, which is our most significant sin, we are unable to see our own sin. It's like trying to fix what is in your head with what is in your head. It cannot be done. We need a power greater than ourselves and outside of ourselves. We need God's help otherwise we are hopeless. This is why we must surrender totally to God (steps 1–3) before we can even think about honestly and humbly looking at ourselves. But if we put all our trust in God, He will reveal our failings to us. He provides the strength we need to humble ourselves, quit the argument and the big lie and get honest with ourselves.

Sin is the central failing of the human condition that is the core subject of every chapter in the Bible. Scripture defines sin as missing the target or falling short of God's standards or failing to obey God. Scripture also claims that we all are sinners. As we have covered over and over in earlier chapters, "There is no one righteous, not even one . . . there is no one who seeks God. All have turned away . . . there is no one who does good, not even one" (Romans 3:10–12). The prophet Isaiah wrote, "We all, like sheep, have gone astray, each of us have turned to our own way; and the Lord has laid on him the iniquity of us all" (Isaiah 53:6). God begins the biblical story of man's salvation with the tragedy that all humans inherit a fallen nature from Adam and Eve that causes them to reject God or create their own God in His place. This new God is often ourselves which is exhibited in our false pride. Simply put, the Bible teaches that we share the original guilt and rebellion of our ancestor, Adam. We are therefore guilty of enjoying our bondage to the world's blatant rebellion against God, to Satan's influence by disregarding God's word and relying on our own natural prideful and selfish desires.

Sin, however, is more than just wrongdoing, sin permeates our total being. It infects our nature at birth and cannot be extracted by deliberate human efforts. Again, the prophet Isaiah illustrates our sinful nature when he cried out in desperation, "Woe is me, for I am lost, for I am a man of unclean lips" (Isaiah 6:5). In the book of Isaiah, King Uzziah was struck down by God with leprosy and was a leper to the day of his death, living in total isolation. Isaiah was most aware of the religious significance of leprosy when he cried out, "I am a man of unclean lips," essentially calling himself a moral leper.

Today, one could consider alcoholism analogous to leprosy in biblical times. It is easy to see the leper as unclean just as it is to see the alcoholic who falls down drunk as unclean. In both cases, we are talking about a spiritual malady, and in both cases, the sinful ways are visible. In a sense, we are all lepers or alcoholics when we see ourselves to be completely lost and broken, covered all over with defilement of sin and entirely corrupt with little or no hope and plead guilty before the Lord. In most cases, our sinful nature is not visible to others due to our ability masterfully cover it up. Nothing is more hopeless and deadly than self-righteousness and self-justification. Because of our pride (self-centeredness), we don't take our sin seriously because we compare ourselves to others by maximizing their wrongs and minimizing our own. But nothing is more hopeful than contrition. Therefore step 4 is all about an honest self-examination of our true natures. Both the Gospel and the twelve steps are about being transformed into the image of God. We are talking about a process of continual spiritual growth, and we will not grow unless we see our need to improve. Hence, an honest self-examination is of paramount importance for spiritual transformation.

The Twelve-Step Program suggests a fearless moral inventory which traditionally has become the first significant obstacle along our path. The twelve-by-twelve says, "Both his pride and fear beat him back every time he tries to look within himself. Pride says, 'You need not pass this way,' and Fear says, 'You dare not look!'" Again, humility and honesty are paramount along with willingness and fearlessness to take this dreaded step. The program suggests we start with the most difficult spiritual sins of pride, and resentment. Step 4 suggest we make a list of the most glaring defects of character, moral failings, maladjustments, wrongdoings or if you will, sins. To avoid confusion, the AA program uses a universally recognized list of human failings—the Seven Deadly Sins of pride, greed, lust, anger, gluttony, envy, and sloth. The twelve-by-twelve states, "It is not by accident that pride heads the procession. For pride, leading to self-justification, and always spurred by conscious or unconscious fears, is the basic breeder of most human difficulties . . . Pride lures us into making demands upon ourselves or upon others which cannot be met without preventing or misusing our God-given instincts."

According to Scripture, the essential iniquity, the ultimate evil, the greatest sin, is Pride. In fact, C. S. Lewis claims in his book *Mere Christianity* that "pride is the great sin." Lewis says, "Unchastity, anger, greed, drunkenness, and all that, are mere fleabites in comparison: it was through Pride that the devil became the devil: Pride leads to every other vice: it is the complete anti-God state of mind." Lewis goes on to say, "But Pride always means enmity . . . and not only enmity between man and man but enmity to God. In God, you come up against something which is in every respect immeasurably superior to yourself. Unless you know God as that—and, therefore, know yourself as nothing in comparison—you do not know God at all. As long as you are proud you cannot know God."

Since we have made the great decision in step 3 to surrender to the process and trust God, God will now give us the humility and honesty to relieve us from the bondage of the Great Sin of Pride. In the Fourth Step, we are asked to write down on paper a fearless moral inventory of ourselves. We begin with our number one killer—resentments. Then we list our fears and sexual immorality. We do this with our sponsor who helps guide us with his experience and pulls our covers when need be. In my case, when I listed this inventory on paper and included what my part was and how it affected my pride alongside each resentment, fear, and sexual misconduct, I begin to see myself for who I was. For the first time in my life, I met my true self. It was not a pleasant experience. In fact, it was often very painful. But as the twelve-by-twelve states, "In every case, pain is the price of admission to a new life."

It is humbling, but as I soon learned, humility is a healer of pain. This is when many of us begin to realize that Humility is the spiritual foundation of all the twelve steps. We also start to understand that it is Humility that is the foundation of God's grace. Having completed this inventory, we are now ready to come clean and admit our faults to both God and our fellows in the fifth step or if you will, confess our sins and repent to God.

Step 5: *Admitted to God, to ourselves, and to another human being the exact nature of our wrongs.*

James 5:16: *"Therefore confess your sins to each other so that you may be healed."*

Luke 23:34: *"Father, forgive them, for they do not know what they are doing."*

Jeremiah 17:9 *"The heart is deceitful above all things and beyond cure."*

John 8:7–11: *"Let any one of you who is without sin be the first to throw a stone at her." "Go now and leave your life of sin."*

Romans 2:15: *"They show that the requirements of the law are written on their hearts, their consciences also bearing witness, and their thoughts sometimes accusing them and at other times even defending them."*

This is the step where we attempt to let go of our struggles, strip ourselves of our pride and admit that we are flat out wrong. It is the time that we quit the cover-up and own up to the exact nature of our wrongs. After years of living a double life, we come clean and admit what we know deep down inside to be true and confess our quilt as charged. As Paul stated in Romans 2:15, "They show that the requirements of the law are written on their hearts, their consciences also bearing witness, and their thoughts sometimes accusing them and at other times even defending them." We have completed our moral inventory in step 4, so it is now time to take out the trash and discard all of the deadwood that is no longer useful. Quit the argument it is finished. God won. Scripture says that God has a plan for our salvation. He has provided a way out—the blood of Christ. All we have to do is let go of the load we have been carrying and nail it to the cross. God plans to justify us through Christ crucified. Jesus cried out on the cross, "Father, forgive them, for they do not know what they are doing" (Luke 23:34).

Humility and honesty are foremost to our conviction. Because of the great sin of pride, it is imperative that we admit our wrongs not only to God and ourselves but another human being. James said, "Therefore confess your sins to each other so that you may be healed" (James 5:16). Let's face it; this is a costly and painful process, and a mentor is imperative not only to guide us but to keep us honest. Bill W. said in his story, "It is not easy; a price has to be paid. It meant the destruction of self-centeredness. I must turn in all things to the Father of light who presides over us all." The human condition is such that it takes a near state of desperation for us to muster up enough courage give up all our rights, strip away our pride and crush our self-centeredness. By pushing our pride aside, we let someone else know the depth of our desperation. In AA, we call this the "Gift of Desperation." In Scripture, this is referred to as "Gift of Tears." So we don't only confess our sins, but we share our sins. As stated earlier, this destruction of self-centeredness and sharing of our sins is tantamount to the coming to the Cross. It is far easier to give what we have than to share what we are. The truth is that you can give up many things, such as your money, your status in life or your work, without affecting your pride. But when you share who you are, without any justification, you strip yourself of your pride. This is the key to enter the new life.

As we stated in chapter 3, repentance is the foundation of Christianity. As Oswald Chambers said, "The entrance into the kingdom of God is through the sharp, sudden pains of repentance colliding with man's respectable 'goodness.' Then the Holy Spirit, who produces these struggles, begins the formation of the Son of God in the person's life." The Big Book suggests that these are revolutionary and drastic proposals, as Bill W. says, "But the moment I fully accepted them, the effect was electric. There was a sense of victory, followed by such a peace and serenity as I have never known."

After taking step 5, the Big Book talks about building a solid spiritual foundation on which we can now continue our walk in confidence with God. We feel the presence of God and receive a sense of peace as our fears slip away. The foundation of our new house has been put solidly into place. We are now ready for God to move in and begin building His palace for Him to live in us. Having come clean, we are now prepared for Steps Six and Seven in which God begins to build a new house.

Chapter VIII

Inside Job: Drop the Rock

Right Sizing (Steps 6 and 7)

Steps 6 and 7 are where we draw upon our willingness and humility in our daily walk with God. Now that we have cleaned our house and given it up to God (steps 4 and 5), the question remains as to whether we are willing to let God enter our house and begin a major renovation project. Having removed any and all barriers that we place in front of God, are we now willing to have God enter us to begin the inside job of transforming our life? In both steps 6 and 7, the emphasis is on what God will accomplish in setting us apart and not on what we can achieve. Our job regarding this life-long endeavor to change our ways from the inside out is to be willing and humble in allowing God to do His work on our behalf. Scripture describes this process as sanctification which means setting us apart onto God for His purpose. Scripture also explains that the Holy Spirit not only gives us a new spiritual life (born again) but also sets us apart to be the possession of Jesus Christ. The claim is that those whom God justifies, the Holy Spirit sanctifies.

C. S. Lewis describes best the work of God to sanctify us in his book *Mere Christianity*: "Imagine yourself as a living house. God comes in to rebuild that house. At first, perhaps, you can understand what He is doing. He is getting the drains right and stopping the leeks in the roof and so on . . . But presently He starts knocking the house about in a way that hurts abominably and does not seem to make sense. What on earth is He up to? He is building quite a different house from the one thought of—throwing out a new wing here, putting on an extra floor there, running up towers, making courtyards. You thought you were going to be made into a decent little cottage: but He is building a palace. He intends to come and live in it Himself."

So it is in step 6 that we are ready to let God have His way with us. We are now willing to let God remove from us those things that we have admitted are objectionable. Then in step 7, we humbly give ourselves to God both the good and the bad and pray for Him to remove our shortcomings. So at this point, we belong to God as His possession to do with us as He will. As Paul wrote to the Corinthians, "You are not your own, for you were bought at a price" (1 Corinthians 6:19–20).

Step 6: *Were entirely ready to have God remove all these defects of character.*

1 Corinthians 6:19–20 *"You are not your own, for you were bought with a price."*

Ephesians 4:22–24: *"You were taught, with regard to your former way of life, to put off your old self, which is being corrupted by deceitful desires; to be made new in the attitude of your minds; and put on the new self."*

Romans 12:2: *"Do not conform to the patterns of this world, but be transformed by the renewing of your mind."*

As we stated earlier in chapter 3, steps 6 and 7 are considered the "hinge" steps of the program, with the first five steps dealing with the removal of obstacles to our relationship with God and the last five steps dealing with repairing our relationship with God and our fellows. According to twelve by twelve, step 6 is "the step that separates the men from the boys." For this is the step for only the most courageous of men to step up and come forward— "without any reservations whatever . . . and sincerely try to grow in the image and likeness of his own creator." We must muster up the courage and willingness by pushing aside self-will and let go by allowing God to have His way—not our way.

Getting entirely ready to allow God to have his way with us may seem simple, but it is not easy. After completing our inventory of defects that need to be discarded and repenting these sins to God in steps four and five, we now must garner the courage to humble ourselves some more and place our trust in God on a daily basis. At this point it is essential to keep in mind the words of scripture, "You were not your own, for you were bought with a price" (1 Corinthians 6:19–20). In other words, we abandon ourselves to God and surrender to Him on a daily basis. This is a lifetime process that doesn't happen overnight. Throughout the Bible, God commands His people to be holy like Him and to strive for perfection. We know, however, that human perfection is not within our reach. Therefore, step six encourages us to press on and strive to obey God's desires for us. If we take on an attitude of willingness and readiness to live a godly life, God will provide us the power to do it. He works in us through the Holy Spirit, giving us the desire and the ability to obey Him.

This is an inside job performed by the Holy Spirit. The process consists of two parts: the gradual removal of our corrupted and polluted human nature and the continuous development of the new life in the likeness of God. "You were taught, with regard to your former way of life, to put off your old self, which is being corrupted by deceitful desires; to be made new in the attitude of your minds; and put on a new self" (Ephesians 4:22–24).

In "My Story," I describe how my life had radically changed. God had entered my heart and soul, and once God grabbed on, He never let go. "He is the peace, hope, freedom and most of all, love." Love is now winning out over fear. It's an inside job. But I had to continually remind myself that it is God that affects the transformation of the new life. He is the one who does the work. I must surrender on a daily basis, thus letting God purify my soul on His terms. Therefore, my job is obedience out of gratitude and yielding the results as God's job. God's gift is a new attitude of gratitude. It is this new attitude of gratitude that begins to strip away the reliance on our prideful ways. We enter what scripture calls our walk with God. We give Him the glory, and we look to Him to show us the way on a daily basis.

Scripture tells us to give up the ways and customs of the world and let God change the way we think. The Bible says, "Do not conform to the patterns of this world, but be transform by the renewing of your mind" (Romans 12:2). Apostle Paul tells us to avoid the ways of the world around us for this thinking will lead us back to our selfish and destructive ways. As we practice the spiritual principles by placing our trust in God, He will work the miracles of changing us from the inside out. As we change on the inside, we begin to exhibit the changes in our outward attitudes and behavior. New freedom takes hold as we seek to do the right thing not because we ought to, but because we want to. The Big Book says, "We will lose interest in selfish things and gain interest in our fellows. Self-seeking will slip away. Our whole attitude and outlook on life will change." In other words, we begin to exhibit true humility. In step 7, we humble ourselves by asking God directly to purify ourselves by removing our shortcomings.

Step 7: *Humbly asked Him to remove our shortcomings.*

Luke 18:14: *"For those exalt themselves will be humbled, and those who humble themselves will be exalted."*

1 John 2:16: *"For everything in the world—the lust of the flesh, the lust of the eyes, and the pride of life—comes not from the Father but from the world. The world and its desires pass away, but whoever does the will of God lives forever."*

Philippians 2:5–9: *"Though he was God . . . he took the humble position of a slave . . . he humbled himself in obedience to God . . . died a criminal's death on a cross . . ."*

The emphasis of step 7 is humility. The definition of humility is the quality or state of not thinking you are better than other people or we don't look down on others as being less than we are. The opposite of humility is pride. As we have discussed earlier, pride is the root of our problems and humility is the solution in that it is the spiritual foundation for both the Gospel and the twelve-step recovery program. This is where we give up all pretense and accept our proper place in our relationship to God and our fellows.

AA uses the term of "right size" to describe our worthiness. Humility is not something that we earn just as we don't earn gratitude; it is something we receive as a gift from God. In fact, gratitude and humility are related in that we are only as humble as we are grateful. Show me a grateful person, and I'll show you a humble person and vice versa. Humility becomes our acceptance of ourselves based on our daily surrender to our all-powerful God.

Also, in step 7 humility seems to be the essential ingredient for transforming pain into spiritual growth. The twelve-by-twelve describes how the constant message of AA reinforced the notion that failure and misery are transformed by humility into new and productive God-centered lives. "We heard story after story of how humility had brought strength out of weakness." The twelve-by-twelve goes on to say, "In every case, pain had been the price of admission into a new life . . . It brought a measure of humility that we soon discovered to be a healer of pain." This is what I experienced in "My Story." When my loving wife described how I had let her and my family down, I felt a piercing emotional pain. It was when I accepted the truth that she was right and I was wrong, could I receive the relief from the excruciating emotional pain. It was only after surrendering to the truth and humbling myself to my God, that God invaded my soul with His grace.

The twelve-by-twelve goes on to say, "Many of us who had thought ourselves religious awoke to the limitations of this attitude . . . But now the words 'Of myself I am nothing, the Father doeth the works' began to carry bright promise and meaning." Hence, the significant turning point in my life came when I finally humbled myself to my God.

Scripture describes throughout the Bible how humility is the foundation of our salvation. As Jesus described in the parable of the Pharisee and Tax Collector, the boastful Pharisee did not find favor before God. But the tax collector admitted his faults and humbly asked for mercy for his sinful ways. Jesus said, "I tell you this sinner, not the Pharisee, returned home justified before God. For those who exalt themselves will be humbled, and those who humble themselves will be exalted" (Luke 18:14) Jesus makes the point clear that we cannot earn our way to salvation. But by coming clean with an honest assessment of our wrongdoings and humbly asking for mercy, we will be justified before God. It is the humble of heart and not the boastful that receive God's favor.

Because of our prideful nature, we tend to hide behind our accomplishments, our status, reputation or the delusion of our self-importance. We spend our efforts in self-justification and constant cover-up which will always drive us to a place of self-centered fear. We live a double life living in constant fear of being found out. We live the big lie and resort to our cowardly ways of running to the bottle to cover it all up. This pattern of self-centered and fear-driven life will eventually lead us into the death spiral. Scripture describes this desire for worldly accomplishment along with the need for self-importance comes not from God but from the evil one. Only by turning away from our lustful ways of human desires and humble ourselves by placing God first in our life, will we receive eternal life with God. "For everything in the world—the lust of the flesh, the lust of the eyes, and the pride of life—comes not from the Father but from the world. The world and its desires pass away, but whoever does the will of God lives forever" (1 John 2:16).

The Gospel of Jesus Christ gives us many examples of humility such as Jesus washing the disciples' feet, riding into

Jerusalem to proclaim Himself the King of King on a donkey to name just a couple. Most importantly, Jesus provides the greatest example in the entire world by paying the ultimate price for our sins on The Cross at Calvary. "Though he was God . . . he took the humble position of a slave . . . he humbled himself in obedience to God . . . died a criminal's death on a cross . . ." (Philippians 2:5–9). In the Big Book, Bill W. makes a feeble attempt to describe this ultimate price to be paid by stating, "Simple but not easy; a price has to be paid. It meant the destruction of self-centeredness. I must turn in all things to the Father of Light who presides over us all.

The Twelve-Step Program talks about "let go and let God." But God can't hand you anything until we let go of what we are holding on to. The question is; what are we holding on to? It's all those accomplishments, our prestige, reputation, and most of all, our pride. This is our rock. These are the things that we have strived for our whole life. Our rock is what we stood for and what we hid behind. But now we begin to see that this so-called rock is not our solid foundation after all. In fact, this is the rock that is holding us down. We find ourselves drowning in a sea of self-centered fear. The program has thrown a lifeline but we can't seem to reach the life preserver. It's my rock that is holding me down. The program screams, "Let it go . . . drop the rock." But I'm hanging on to the rock . . . "It's my rock, and I can't let go." This is the core of the twelve steps . . . We must let go . . . We must drop the rock. God can't hand us His gift of grace until we drop what we are holding on to. "Drop the rock!"

When we come to God with empty hands, He will extend His hand with love, mercy, and grace. Our old discarded rock consisted of self-centered fear, while our new foundation is the love of God. When we drop the rock, we quit acting out of fear and begin serving out of love. As we start to act more and more out of love, we become more useful to God's purpose. The program helps us see our fears and face up to them with God's help. Before I was oblivious to my fears and even worse than that, I ran from them via the bottle. I couldn't cope with my fears and took the cowards way out through drinking.

Through the program, I receive the courage that I need to face my fears with the love of God. The program also suggests that if we don't feel the love, act as if we do and eventually God's love will drive our behavior. "Act as if, or fake it until we make it" is the AA adage. **Illustration 3** depicts the process of the renewing of our mind through the action steps of six and seven. The seventh step suggests that we don't "think" our way into good living, we "live" our way into good thinking.

Again, the twelve step program is an action plan. It is only by taking action and changing our behavior do we grow in spirit. As James says, "Do not merely listen to the word, and so deceive yourselves. Do what it says" (James 1: 22). As **Illustration 3** delineates, the 'New Way' is to change our behavior (or act 'as if') which will change our feelings and then in turn our thinking will change. In other words, we will experience a renewing of the mind. The 'Old Way' is to start by thinking about it or just change your thinking on your own. The old way doesn't work because we can't change what is in our head with what is in our head. Put another way, we can live ourselves into good thinking, but we can't think ourselves into good living.

Illustration 3

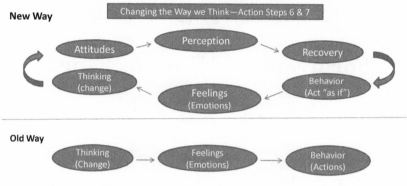

Renewing of the Mind

Do not conform to the pattern of this world, but be transformed by the renewing of your mind. (Romans 12: 2)

Notes:
1. We don't think our way into good living, we live our way into good thinking.
2. Act "as If".
3. By changing the way we Act (behavior), Our feelings change, which in turn changes the way we think.
4. We can't change what is in our head (thinking) with what is in our head.

Finally, the Big Book describes in what we call the seventh step prayer how acting out of love, we become useful to God's purpose, as follows: "My creator, I am now willing that you should have all of me, good and bad. I pray that you now remove from me every single defect of character which stands in the way of my usefulness to you and my fellows. Grant me strength, as I go out from here to do your bidding." We have completed step 7, and we are now ready for more action. "Faith without works is dead." Let's look at steps 8 and 9.

CHAPTER IX

———❦———

Forgiveness: Minding Fences

Repairing Relationships *(Steps 8 and 9)*

We spoke in the last chapter about steps 6 and 7 representing the hinge steps. The first five steps deal with removing barriers to our relationship with God and our fellows, while the last five steps deal with repairing these relationships. In step 4 we discovered that we suffer from brokenness in our lives concerning both our relationship with God as well as our relationships with others. In the Twelve-Step Recovery Program, our brokenness tends to weight us down and lead us back to our addictions. Central to ongoing recovery is to mend these broken relationships.

Giving and receiving forgiveness is an essential part of the healing process regarding our broken relationships. Forgiveness requires that we make peace with God, within ourselves, and with those that we have wronged. The central truth is that we must forgive to be forgiven and this can't be accomplished without God playing the central role. God's forgiveness of us and our forgiveness of others go hand-in-hand together. Jesus said, "That if we refuse to forgive others, God will not forgive our sins" (Matthew 6:14–15).

Steps 8 and 9 are concerned with repairing broken personal relationships. Taking these actions is not a simple process. It's not just a matter of apologizing or claiming that we are sorry. Most of the people that we have hurt are tired of hearing that we were sorry over and over again. The Big Book refers to both of these steps as making "amends." The amends process consists of three elements. First, we must identify to who we were at fault and own up to our part. Next, we make a vigorous attempt to repair the damage done. Finally, we provide evidence of how we have changed our ways not to make this mistake again. In other words, we need to (1) admit that we knocked our neighbor's fence down, (2) then repair the fence, and (3) explain what we have changed so that we don't continue to knock their fence down. To accomplish this most important and challenging task, we must come with a forgiving heart.

Step 8: *"Made a list of all persons we had harmed and became willing to make amends to them all."*

1 John 4:20: *"Whoever claims to love God yet hates a brother and sister is a liar. For whoever does not love their brother or sister, whom they have seen, cannot love God, whom they have not seen."*

Step 8 consists of two parts. First, we identify those who we have wronged, and secondly, we become willing to make amends to them all. For various reasons, we may not be able to make amends to certain people, but this step demands that we be honestly willing to make amends if the opportunity presents itself.

The first part of step 8 is not very difficult for most of the work has already been accomplished if we did a thorough step 4. The fourth step inventory provides a list of the people we have harmed. In step 8 we merely pare this list down to those people where we need to set things right to clear our conscience. However, becoming willing to make amends to them all is another matter altogether. In this case, we must review our part, own up to it and be willing to make every effort to repair the damage done.

Before taking action in step 9, let's define the action word *amend*. *Webster's Dictionary* defines it as follows: "To make better; to repair, restore; to free from faults; put right, correct, rectify . . . to change or modify in any way for the better; to recover from illness." This definition fits like a glove for the AA Recovery Program. Our program is all about recovering from an illness by restoring to sanity, putting things right, and repairing the damage.

The question remains; why is it so crucial to our recovery to go back and make an effort to repair our relationships? The answer for the alcoholic is simple; if personal relationships are not repaired, we will most likely drink. Hence, making amends are essential to achieving long-term sobriety. Scripture also speaks to the necessity to love our brothers to love God. John says in 1 John 4:20-21, "Whoever claims to love God yet hate a brother and sister is a liar. For whoever does not love their brother and sister, whom they have seen, cannot love God, whom they have not seen. And he has given us this command: Anyone who loves God must also love their brother and sister." In other words, there is connectivity that runs through God, ourselves, and other people. If there is any blockage in this current of connectivity, the circuit will be broken. Therefore, living in touch with God, having a successful contact and relationship with Him is inextricably bound up with human relationships. Rev. Sam Shoemaker said it best, "We cannot stay in touch with

God without righting the human relationships. This is the law of love in action. We love because He first loved us."

Step 9: *"Made direct amends to such people wherever possible, except when to do so would injure them or others."*

   Colossians 3:13: *"Bear with each other and forgive one another if any of you has a grievance against someone. Forgive as the Lord forgave you."*

   Matthew 5:23–24: *"Therefore, if you are offering your gift at the altar and that your brother or sister has something against you leave your gift there in front of the altar. First, go and be reconciled to them; then come and offer your gift."*

   Matthew 6:14–15: *"If you forgive those who sin against you, your heavenly Father will forgive you. But if you refuse to forgive others, your Father will not forgive your sins."*

Making actual amends is not easy. In fact, it is one of the most challenging step of the program, but it is also one of the most rewarding. Step 9 is also referred to as "the dreaded ninth step," but it is necessary if we are to stay sober. We just cannot continue to carry the baggage of anger, resentments, and self-pity any longer, or it will kill us.

To grow spirituality and to make progress, it is essential that we take action regarding our personal inventory and make amends to the people we have hurt. This involves shedding our self-justification and being honest about our failures and humbling ourselves to our God. Apostle Paul in his letter to the Colossians says in 3:13, "Bear with each other and forgive one another if any of you has a grievance against someone. Forgive as the Lord forgave you."

Step 9 says that we must make amends where necessary, seek forgiveness from those we have hurt and forgive those who have injured us. We must drop the rock! If we don't, it will drag us down. This is where we take responsibility, own up to our part, make amends, and thus clean up our side of the street. This is easier said than done. But at this stage of our development, we have developed some of the spiritual courage necessary for God to help us through. At this point, we have received the spiritual tools of humility and forgiveness to move forward to repair relationships with our fellows.

In most cases, when making amends, we are asking for forgiveness. But in many cases, we must be willing to forgive to be forgiven. Jesus teaches that you must forgive to be forgiven. "If you forgive those who sin against you, your heavenly Father will forgive you. But if you refuse to forgive others, your Father will not forgive your sins." Hence, true forgiveness is an essential part of our recovery program and our pathway to truth. And of course, none of this is even possible without God's help which means we must humble ourselves to our God. It is often said, "I believe that I can forgive others, but I have a hard time forgiving myself." We must guard against this kind of prideful thinking for Jesus said that we must forgive to be forgiven. Only God Himself can forgive us; hence we must humble ourselves to God and focus on forgiving others to be forgiven.

There is another spiritual truth regarding forgiveness that can be most difficult to overcome. The twelve-by-twelve states, "It is a spiritual axiom that every time we are disturbed, no matter what the cause, there is something wrong with us. If somebody hurts us and we are sore, we are in the wrong also." The twelve-by-twelve goes on to say that there are no exceptions.

Justifiable anger and resentments are not allowed. Now, this does not seem fair. When we are wronged, we must look for our part and be willing to make amends? Is this possible, we ask? It is not only possible but required if we are to be forgiven. This is tantamount to Jesus saying in Matthew 5:44: "Love your enemies and pray for those who persecute you . . ." This seems near impossible to do, and it is, without God's help.

Jesus taught, "Therefore, if you are offering your gift at the altar and that your brother or sister has something against you, leave your gift there in front of the altar. First, go and be reconciled to them; then come and offer your gift." This is an essential process to repair the brokenness, shame, and guilt that we have suffered. I know that in "My Story," it was not so much about the guilt of what I had done, but about what I had not done. It was more about how I had let my loved ones down. It took the spiritual tools of prayer, humility, and forgiveness for me to quit the self-justification and let God begin the healing process.

A huge weight was lifted from my shoulders. Our purpose is to place ourselves in a position to be of maximum service to God and the people about us. The old man is dead, and the new man comes alive. Paul says in Colossians 3:12–15, "Since God chose you to be the holy people he loves, you must clothe yourselves with compassion, kindness, humility, gentleness, and patience . . . and over all these virtues put on love . . . let the peace of Christ rule in your hearts, since as members of one body you were called to peace."

These words from Apostle Paul sound similar to what the Big Book refers to as the promises of the twelve-step program when we begin making amends in step 9, "If we are painstaking about this phase of our development, we will be amazed before we are halfway through. We are going to know a new freedom and a new happiness. We will not regret the past nor wish to shut the door on it. We will comprehend the word serenity, and we will know peace. No matter how far down the scale we have gone, we will see how our experience can benefit others. That feeling of uselessness and self-pity will disappear. We will lose interest in selfish things and gain interest in our fellows. Self-seeking will slip away. Our whole attitude and outlook upon life will change. Fear of people and economic insecurity will leave us. We will intuitively know how to handle situations which used to baffle us. We will suddenly realize that God is doing for us what we could not do for ourselves . . . Are these extravagant promises? We think not. They are being fulfilled among us— sometimes quickly, sometimes slowly. They will always materialize if we work for them."

After starting the amends process, the Big Book suggests that we should begin working step 10, which is a process of daily living.

CHAPTER X

Daily Bread (*Step 10*)

Step 10 captures the concept of "one day at a time" along with the idea of self-examination on a daily basis. This step suggests that we need daily spiritual nourishment to continue our journey of spiritual development. Step 10 is a work in progress that will last a lifetime. As the Big Book says, "We claim spiritual progress rather spiritual perfection." The Big Book also cautions us to not . . . "let up on the spiritual program of action and rest on our laurels." This step stresses a program of action consisting of both discipline and perseverance. As James says, "Do not merely listen to the word . . . do what it says" (James 1:22). Now that we have cleaned our own house in steps 4 through 9, we are now ready to keep a clean house by monitoring our character defects and their consequences through a daily inventory and taking prompt corrective action as needed.

Step 10: *"Continued to take personal inventory and when we were wrong promptly admitted it."*

James 1:22: *"Do not merely listen to the word, and so deceive yourself. Do what it says."*

1 Timothy 4:7–8: *"Have nothing to do with godless myths and old wives' tales; rather, train yourself to be godly. For physical training is of some value, but godliness has value for all things, holding promise for both the present life and the life to come."*

2 Timothy 2:3: *"Join with me in suffering, like a good soldier of Jesus Christ."*

1 John 1:8–9: *"If we claim to have no sin, we are only fooling ourselves and not living in the truth. But if we confess our sins, He is faithful and just to forgive our sins and cleanse us from all unrighteousness."*

Step 10 comprises steps 4 through 9 in a comprehensive package to be applied in our daily lives. In other words, it is a design for living on a daily basis. The Big Book says, "When we retire at night, we constructively review our day . . . On awakening let us think about the twenty-four hours ahead . . . Before we begin, we ask God to direct our thinking, especially asking that it be divorced from self-pity, dishonest or self-seeking motives."

Step 10 is applied daily for it is never completed. This step requires self-discipline with continued perseverance to keep our pride and self-will in check. There is no time to rest on our laurels; we must continue to grow and move forward by taking action and more action.

Scripture is also very explicit in stating that action is a requirement. The book of James states that we must do what the word says and that faith without works is dead. James says,

"Do not merely listen to the word, and so deceive yourselves . . . do what it says. Anyone who listens to the word but does not do what says is like someone who looks at his face in the mirror . . . goes away and immediately forgets what he looks like. But whoever looks intently into the perfect law . . . not forgetting what they have heard, but doing it—they will be blessed in what they do" (James 1:22-25).

These words demonstrate how the Bible emphasizes the application of the truth versus just obtaining the knowledge of the truth. In fact, relying on our intellect for our spiritual truth may do harm to our spiritual growth. It happens too often for the intellectual to be most opposed to Jesus Christ. Saul is undoubtedly illuminative example of one of the most knowledgeable Pharisees living during Jesus life but was blind to the truth of Christ Jesus. It was not until he was struck blind by God that Saul was able to begin his walk in the truth and the light by being filled with the Holy Spirit. The story of Saul illustrates that it is not so much our intellect but our actions of making a routine examination of our life and take immediate action to correct ourselves when we see that we have gone off the rails.

This step suggests, "When we were wrong promptly admitted it." After looking in the mirror and seeing mustard on our face, it would be foolish to go all day without wiping our face clean. Hence, step 10 claims that if we don't examine our actions daily and take corrective action immediately, we subject ourselves to a fall. Honest, accurate self-examination and personal inventory of our spiritual state are crucial. Jesus says, "If someone claims, 'I know God,' but doesn't obey his commandments, that person is a liar and is not living in the truth" (1 John 2:4–5). To live a Godly life on a daily basis takes a tremendous amount of discipline.

With a nature of self-centeredness, it is more than difficult to submit to God's will all the time. Hence, it takes a rigorous training program to stay on the rails and consistently receive our daily bread by living a God-centered life. How can this be done? The only chance we have is by looking to God for help first thing upon awakening each day. C. S. Lewis describes the difficulty of living the God-centered life which comes to us each morning the moment we wake up. "All your wishes and hopes for the day rush at you like wild animals. And the first job each morning consists simply shoving them all back . . . letting that other larger, stronger, quieter life come flowing in . . . Standing back from all your natural fussing and fretting."

In other words, we push aside our old way of coping and let our new life flow in by letting Him work in us. Lewis says, "We can only do it for moments at first. But from those moments the new sort of life will be spreading through our system." Instead of being self-reliant, we become God-reliant. However, this takes practice just like anything that doesn't come naturally to us. Even if we are a natural, we must practice becoming proficient at those things that are new to us. We must take baby steps first before we begin to run. The same practice, training, and discipline must be applied in our spiritual development as we exercise in our physical and mental development. This practice program consists of examining the results of our actions against some norm of expectation. We then replicate those actions that achieve positive results and try to discard those actions that bring about adverse effects.

The Bible speaks about admitting our wrongs to others and confessing our sins to God. However, it seems so difficult to continually come to God with the same unintentional sins of pride, anger, selfishness, worry, and a whole host of sins that seem to recur daily. Therefore, it is easier to push these sins aside as if God will not notice. But, God sees everything for there is no hiding from Him as Adam and Eve attempted to do in the Garden. Hence, we must come out of hiding and come clean every day. Scripture claims that if we repent, God will forgive us. The apostle John says, "If we claim to have no sin, we are only fooling ourselves and not living in the truth. But if we confess our sins, He is faithful and just to forgive our sins and cleanse us from all unrighteousness" (1 John 1:8–9). Through this daily practice of examining all our wrongdoings and confessing our sins to God, our relationship with God grows stronger, and our actions will show it.

The most difficult spiritual principle to accept is the axiom in step 10 of the twelve-by-twelve that claims, "Every time we are disturbed, no matter what the cause, there is something wrong with us. If someone hurts us and we are sore, we are in the wrong also." The program says that there is no exceptions, not even justifiable anger. This principle just doesn't seem fair. But in the spiritual realm, it is not about fairness; it is about serenity. It is all too often that we are annoyed by other people's shortcomings as if we don't have any.

Whatever the case, we suggest taking a quick daily inventory of our ups and downs. As our inventory itemizes our disturbances, we are advised to exercise four necessary actions. First, apply self-restraint. Second, willing to admit it when the fault is ours. Third, forgive when the blame falls on others. And finally, don't be discouraged when we fall into the errors of our old ways. Because these disciplines are not natural, we should seek progress and not perfection.

It is not easy for us to admit our wrongs or forgive others for the harm done to us. But the Bible tells us to repent and forgive to be forgiven. The truth of the Gospel tells us about the enormous spiritual debt we have to God with no means of repayment. Our debts have been paid in full by Christ crucified. We have nothing to offer but our sins. All we need to do is to nail our sins to the cross by admitting our wrongs and placing our trust in Him. Admitting our mistakes is a daily discipline. By putting our faith in Him, we allow things to happen without striving to predict or control the outcomes. We relax in the presence of the light of His everlasting love.

When we project our self into the future trying to control the outcome, we are seeking self-sufficiency and trying to be adequate without His help. Autonomy is such a subtle sin which is so familiar that it is rarely noticed. Therefore, the alternative is to live in the present by training our mind to seek God's help continually, even when we feel competent to handle the situation before us. We learn to rely on God in every case. This discipline allows us to be more at peace and continue to grow daily in the light of the spirit. "But if we walk in the light . . . Jesus purifies us from all sin" (1 John 1:7). The answer is obedience to God's will, and the relationship is immediately strengthened.

In "My Story" I spoke about the gift of a loving God that was so freely given to me. This is the gift of gratitude, forgiveness, and love. This did not come about through study or trying harder, but by submitting to God and becoming obedient to God. This discipline and obedience became a daily process of surrender to God and asking for His help every day. Through prayer, I ask God to help in five significant areas of my life:

1. Live in the present, one day at a time; don't regret the past or worry about the future. I used to continually project most everything out into the future and worry about it. Today, I replace my worries with prayer. It is only in the present state that I can connect to my infinite God.

2. An attitude of gratitude: always give glory to God for He provides everything.

3. Trust God by abandoning myself to Him: third step

   a) Surrender to the process (my job).
   b) Let go and give up the results to Him (His job).

4. Love my fellows: look for the good in the sinner and not sin in the saint. Be of service, teachable, forgiving, and praise others.

5. Live life on life's terms . . . and accept this sinful world as it is, as He did, not as I would have it.

As you can see from the above disciplines, this is a program of action based on daily obedience to God. Through this obedience, God opens up the heavens and continually reveals His truth that will set you free. Oswald Chambers observes, "God will never reveal more truth about Himself to you until you obey what you already know." Hence, the key to daily spiritual growth is obedience. We turn now to the next discipline which is increasing our conscious contact with God through Prayer and meditation.

CHAPTER XI

Prayer, Love, and Spiritual Awakening (*Steps 11–12*)

1. Prayer (Step 11) Conscious Contact with God

Step 11 is one of the essential elements in the continuing nourishment of our spiritual condition. Without prayer, our relationship with our Father is unable to flourish. However, even as "children of God" prayer is the most difficult thing to do. The problem is the restless mind that tends to focus our idle thoughts on self-absorption. The Big Book defines prayer as "the raising of the heart and mind to God—and in this sense includes meditation." The Bible speaks of prayer as the way we commune with God, and the Big Book speaks of our conscious contact with God.

Step 11: *"Sought through prayer and meditation to improve our conscious contact with God as we understand Him, praying only for knowledge of His will for us and the power to carry that out."*

Matthew 6:6: *"When you pray, go into your room, and when you have shut your door, pray to your Father who is in the secret place . . ."*

Luke 11:1: *"One of His disciples said to Him, 'Lord, teach us to pray . . ."*

Philippians 4:5–6: *"Don't worry about anything; instead pray about everything. Tell God what you need, and thank Him for what He has done. Then you will experience God's peace, which exceeds anything we can understand. His peace will guard your hearts and minds as you live in Jesus Christ."*

Romans 8:26: *"We do not know what to pray for as we ought, but the Spirit himself intercedes for us with groanings too deep for words."*

Both scripture and the Big Book claim that prayer is essential in developing a continuing relationship with God and they both acknowledge its difficulty. Prayer indeed is not typical for the natural man. But it is even a struggle for the "born again" child of God. The natural man looks upon prayer as a means of merely getting the things he wants in life. But the Bible makes clear that the purpose of prayer is to get to know God and His well for us. Step 11 in the Big Book says that "Prayer, as commonly understood, is a petition to God . . . to improve our conscious contact with God . . . praying only for knowledge of His will for us and the power to carry that out."

When the disciples asked Jesus to teach them to pray, Jesus offered the "Lord's Prayer" as a model of how to pray consisting of; adoration and reverence for God, bear our souls in confession, express gratitude and thanksgiving for what He provides for us, and offering a petition for our needs. As Matthew says, we must pray to God who is in a secret place or to address God alone and not to some figure of idolatry. Most important, we come to God in willful submission with sincerity and reverence.

Step 11, stress that we should always pray for the knowledge of His will and the power to carry that out. The twelve steps also claim that we have found tremendous power and results beyond question through their knowledge and experience. The twelve-by-twelve says, "All those who have persisted have found the strength not ordinarily their own. They have wisdom beyond their usual capability. And they have increasingly found a peace of mind which can stand firm in the face of difficult circumstances." Finding peace of mind is consistent with the Bible which says in Philippians 4:6, "Then you will experience God's peace, which exceeds anything we can understand." The biblical power of prayer is not so much to change things but to change us. In other words, our harden hearts are softened by prayer.

The Bible claims that prayer is an effort of the will and as we stated earlier, it is challenging for us to do. Because of our prideful, self-centered ways, it is an arduous task to focus our minds on what is essential in God's eyes versus straying off to daily wondering thoughts. Jesus suggests that we find a private place where we can focus on Him. "When you pray, go into your room, and when you have shut your door, pray to your Father who is in the secret place . . . and he will reward you openly" (Matthew 6:6).

Jesus says, "Shut your door." We shut the door on our hardened heart and open ourselves to Him who softens our heart. God's word encourages us to get into the habit of dealing with Him about everything. Step 11 helps us to open up our lives to God the first thing every morning which has proven to get us on the right track each new day. Unless we learn this, we will be working from the wrong level throughout the day. The Big Book says, "On awakening let us think about the twenty-four hours ahead . . . before we begin, we ask God to direct our thinking, especially asking that it be divorced from self-pity, dishonest or self-seeking motives . . . our thought life will be placed on a much higher plane when our thinking is cleared of wrong motives."

Step 11 is a very practical step. The twelve-by-twelve says, "Almost the only scoffers at prayer are those who never tried it enough." Therefore, prayer is merely an exercise in ongoing practice. It may seem awkward at first, but God will make it easier as we practice the discipline of prayer. Hence, prayer is our spiritual nourishment like food, air, and sunshine. If we should deprive ourselves of this essential nourishment of prayer, our soul will suffer just as the body will if it doesn't receive daily water, food and air.

Throughout scripture, the idea of prayer is to humble ourselves to God and in essence become God-reliant vs. self-reliant. In being God-reliant, we do ask for those things He can do for us and what we cannot do for ourselves. In our natural life, we ask for very few things because it is our nature to be self-reliant. The Bible suggests that we ask like little children, for children know that they are dependent upon their parents. Jesus says, "Unless you change and become like little children, you will never enter the kingdom of heaven" (Matthew 18:3). In "My Story," I spoke of my being self-reliant as a virtue in my life. I saw prayer as foolishness. Little did I know that this way of thinking was the cause of my spiritual malady, namely— self-centered fear!

Therefore, we need to learn to ask for those things that we cannot do for ourselves. The Bible says, "Ask, and you will receive . . ." (John 16:24). We need to give Jesus Christ the room to work His miracles in us. The problem is that we are unable to do this until we have reached the bitter end. It is when we have reached this state of total desperation, are we able muster up the courage to pray. And God says, "Don't worry about anything; instead pray about everything. Tell God what you need, and thank Him for what He has done. Then you will experience God's peace, which exceeds anything we can understand. His peace will guard your hearts and minds as you live in Jesus Christ" (Philippians 4:5–6). The twelve steps claim that we find great strength, wisdom, and peace through prayer. The twelve-by-twelve says, "All those who have persisted have found the strength not ordinarily their own. They have found wisdom beyond their usual capability. And they have increasingly found a peace of mind which can stand firm in the face of difficult circumstances."

Both the Bible and the twelve steps insist that prayer gives us a great sense of belonging to God in His kingdom. The twelve-by-twelve says, "We no longer live in a completely hostile world. We are no longer lost and frightened and purposeless. The moment we catch even a glimpse of God's will, the moment we begin to see truth, justice, and love as the real and eternal things in life, we are no longer deeply disturbed by all the seeming evidence to the contrary that surrounds us in purely human affairs. We know that God lovingly watches over us. We know that when we turn to Him, all will be well with us, here and hereafter." After reading this comforting excerpt from step 11, we now turn to step 12 where we give it away with love.

2. Love (Step 12): Giving It Away

Step 12 is all about being of service and helping our fellows with love find their way to freedom through faith in God. It is God's will that we love others. Love is more than a feeling that we are unable to explain; it is choosing to behave in a caring and loving way. With God's grace, His love grows in us as we place our trust in Him.

Step 12: *"Having had a spiritual awakening as the result of these steps, we tried to carry this message to alcoholics, and to practice these principles in all our affairs."*

1 John 4:7–8 *"Dear friends, let us continue to love one another, for love comes from God. Anyone who loves is a child of God and knows God. But anyone who does not love does not know God, for God is love."*

The most crucial element in our journey to the truth is "Love." In fact, Apostle Paul says in 1 Corinthians 13:13, "And now these three remain faith, hope, and love. But the greatest of these is love." The Big Book claims that this love is a gift from God and if we are to keep it, we must give it away. We demonstrate this gift of love by serving others with a helping hand. The Bible says that we serve God by being the servants of others. Service is the principal theme of step 12. The twelfth step says, "Freely ye have received; freely give" is the core of this part step 12. The twelve-by-twelve describes the great joy and satisfaction of a twelve-step job well done.

"To watch the eyes of men and women open with wonder as they move from darkness into light, to see their lives quickly fill with new purpose and meaning . . . and above all to watch these people awaken to the presence of a loving God in their lives—these things are the substance of what we receive as we carry AA's message to the next alcoholic." Jesus said, "The greatest among you must be a servant. But those who exalt themselves will be humbled, and those who humble themselves will be exalted" (Matthew 23:11–12).

Step 12 says, "Having had a spiritual awakening as the result of these steps, we tried to carry this message to alcoholics, and practice these principles in all of our affairs." In other words, having received the gift of grace from a loving God, we must give it away to keep it. Scripture says that by the grace of God, we have been filled with His Holy Spirit. "But you will receive power when the Holy Spirit comes on you; and you will be my witnesses in Jerusalem . . . and to the ends of the earth (Acts 1:8)."

Having worked the twelve steps, we are in a special position to carry the message to others. We identify with those who are suffering the difficulties of the trials that we have suffered. With God's help, we extend our hand to those who seek help and place their hand into the hand of God. In helping others in such deep and sensitive issues, we speak in the language of love, not condemnation. The Bible tells us, "If someone is caught in a sin, you who live by the Spirit should restore that person gently . . . Share each other's burdens, and in this way, you will fulfill the law of Christ" (Galatians 6:1–2).

Christ commanded us to "Love one another. As I have loved you, so you must love one another" (John 13:34). "There is no greater love than to lay down one's life for one's friends" (John 15:13). As we work the twelfth step, we are not the Savior, but we can love others as He has loved us. Love doesn't just deal with the problems, but it helps carry the weight of the burdens. We become part of a support network to help carry our friends until they can take steps on their own toward recovery. Step 12 suggests that we carry the message not by explaining the way, but by sharing our own story of experience, strength, and hope.

3. Spiritual Awakening

Romans 8:8–14: *"Those who are in the realm of the flesh cannot please God. You, however, are not in the realm of the flesh but are in the realm of the Spirit, if indeed the Spirit of God lives in you . . . for those who are led by the Spirit of God are children of God."*

The twelfth step principle begins by stating, "Having had a spiritual awakening as *the* result of these steps . . ." It does not say "as *a* result . . ." What seems to be a minimal difference between these two statements is very significant. The twelfth step statement is making it clear that the sole purpose of the Twelve-Step Program is to achieve a spiritual awakening. A spiritual awakening is not simply one of many gifts of the program, but it is the sole purpose of the twelve-step action plan. In fact, it was this spiritual awakening that revealed the presence of God in my life and led me to a personal relationship with Jesus through the Gospel of Jesus Christ. Both the Bible and the Big Book disavowal any notion that the pathway to truth is gained by an intellectual exercise. In the Bible, Jesus says that we must receive the kingdom of God like a little child. The Big Book maintains that a spiritual awakening will come about as a result of practicing action steps vs. an intellectual exercise. The Big Book defines the spiritual awakening "as a new state-of-consciousness and being . . . or an awareness of a power greater than ourselves." In either case, we do not receive God's presence through a hardened intellectual exercise but by a softening of our heart.

The miracle of the AA program rests solidly on the foundation of this gift of a new life through a spiritual awakening as the result of working the twelve steps. In fact, the Big Book says in chapter 2, "There Is a Solution," "The great fact is just this, and nothing less: That we have had deep and effective spiritual experiences which have revolutionized our whole attitude toward life toward our fellows and toward God's universe. The central fact of our lives today is the absolute certainty that our Creator has entered into our hearts and lives in a way which is indeed miraculous. He has commenced to accomplish those things for us which we could never do by ourselves."

The Big Book describes the beginning of the spiritual awakening in step 3 "as we become conscious of His presence, we begin to lose our fear . . . We were reborn." The Bible says that we must be "born again" to enter the kingdom of God. "Jesus replied, Very truly I tell you, no one can see the kingdom of God unless they are born again" (John 3:3) In both cases, we receive a new life, a spiritual life through the spirit of God in us. Without the spirit of God in us, we remain lost and unable to find our way.

The Bible speaks about the spiritual blindness that renders us incapable of grasping our need for God's help. Without this recognition and the guidance of God through His spirit, we will not comprehend the Bible. We may think that we grasp the Word, but it will remain veiled. It was when I became alive to God as the result of the Holy Spirit's work that I was able to receive His Word in the Bible. Before my heart and soul were invaded by the Holy Spirit, and I was born again, the Bible did not come alive to me. I was unable to relate to the Bible personally.

When I read the Bible now, I know without any doubt that God is speaking to me personally. Apostle Paul says in 1 Corinthian 2:14, "The man without the Spirit does not accept the things that come from the Spirit of God, for they are foolishness to him, and he cannot understand them because they are spiritually discerned." Both the Bible and the twelve steps maintain that we must be Born Again. Before we were born again, we may have known and perhaps believed some theological facts, but God was not real to our innermost self.

The Big Book says, "Many of us had moral and philosophical convictions galore, but we could not live up to them even though we would have liked to." In other words, we don't think our way into a godly relationship, and we will not see the truth through an intellectual exercise. The truth is revealed to us by process of letting go of everything that we held close to ourselves. We let go of our old way of thinking and surrendered to the process. We realized that we could not fix what was in our head with what was in our head. The Big Book says, "Neither could we reduce our self-centeredness much by wishing or trying on our own power. We had to have God's help."

The Bible explains that once we are invaded by the Holy Spirit, we no longer live in the realm of the flesh, but in the realm of the spirit. It is only through God's work that we live in the realm of the Spirit, and the Spirit lives in us. The Bible also makes clear that we not only are alive in God by the Holy Spirit, but we are alive in God's Word of the Bible. Without the Spirit of God in us, we are unable to discern the truth of God's Word. Therefore, the key to our new life as God's child is to surrender to the process that delivers a spiritual awakening which leads to the revelation of the Gospel of Jesus Christ.

CHAPTER XII

Victory—GOD WON

Having now gone through the twelve steps of Alcoholics Anonymous and reflected on how each step has been primarily derived directly from the Gospel; we are struck by the many similarities and the absence of any significant differences. The Big Book claims that the twelve steps are a set of principles that act as a guide for spiritual progress and not a claim of spiritual perfection. The Big Book states that the twelve steps make clear . . . "Three pertinent ideas:

(a) That we were alcoholic and could not manage our own lives.
(b) That probably no human power could have relieved our alcoholism.
(c) That God could and would if He were sought."

If the words "alcoholic and alcoholism" are replaced with the words "sinners and sinful ways," then we begin to see how the relevant ideas of the twelve steps apply directly to the core truth of the Gospel. The Big Book describes "alcoholism" as merely the symptom of the problem with the root cause being a spiritual malady. In other words, our predicament consists of the depravity of sinful pride. This very much parallels the basic principles of the Christian worldview described by many theologians, which are the following:

(a) Creation . . . made in His image.
(b) The Fall . . . turning away from our creator and falling into a sinful cursed world.
(c) Grace . . . God as our savior through Christ crucified.
(d) Glory . . . God fulfilling His purpose through the supremacy of His Son Christ Jesus over the everlasting kingdom of God.

The obvious distinction is that the twelve steps do not call out the name of Jesus Christ as the Son of God and does not describe the necessary destruction of self-centeredness as Christ crucified. Never the less, the twelve steps do state that we do need to be "reborn" just as Jesus explained to Nicodemus that we must be "born again" in order to enter the Kingdom of God. As described in "My Story," it was in step 3 that God came to my rescue. I had come to believe that I needed a power greater than myself to restore me to sanity in step 2, but I struggled in step 3 with the idea of placing all my trust in God. Furthermore, at that time I was not necessarily seeking God through a belief in Jesus Christ. In fact, I was in a desperate state of mind. I was now seeking help from God but struggling with the surrender of my will to God. To give up control was so foreign to me for my nature was to be in charge. Remember, self-reliance was what I considered to be my greatest virtue.

The great irony is that my so called virtue of self-reliance became the core of the problem. The drinking problem was but a symptom of the disease. The root cause of the disease was self-centered fear, or if you will, my prideful sinful nature which the Big Book calls a "spiritual malady." Hence, it was the idea of the third step of simply making a decision to turn my will and my life over to the care of God that made all the difference for me. As I described in "My Story," it was when I put all the chips on the table and made the decision that I'm all in; that is when God showed up in my life. Again, I wasn't necessarily seeking Jesus Christ, but I was making a choice to surrender to the process of letting God in. I can't explain it.

There may be no explanation, but I do believe there is a formulation that works—the twelve steps of Alcoholics Anonymous. As the Big Book explains it in the third step, "First of all, we had to quit playing God. It didn't work. Next we decided . . . God was going to be our director . . . He is the Father, and we are His children. Most good ideas are simple, and this concept was the keystone of the new and triumphant arch through which we passed to freedom." This was my first attempt to let God in and strip away the self-will, which always blocked His entry into my life. I did not see it at the time, but looking back, it is clear that this is when God invaded my heart and soul and begin doing for me what I could not do for myself.

God has been carrying me or should I say guiding me and nudging me ever since. Suddenly, I realized that my old attitude of entitlement had been transformed into an attitude of gratitude. God had enabled me to get honest with myself and quit engaging in the big lie of self-justification. Let me be clear, God's grace did not arrive *by what I did*, but *because of what I did* . . . namely, abandoning myself to Him. God says, "Seek me and you will find me" (Matthew 7:8). However, when God invaded my heart and soul and grabbed on, He never let go. I was "reborn" or if you will "born again" and have been led by the Holy Spirit ever since.

By the grace of God, everything changed. I was led back to church, but this time to praise and worship God versus going to church because it is expected of a good Christian. The Word of God became alive to me and "the scales of prejudice fell from my eyes." Soon after working the third Step, I was baptized at my church to publicly display my belief in the Father, Son, and the Holy Spirit. I began reading daily devotionals, the Bible, Christian literature, I joined small Bible study groups, and began helping and serving others in the AA fellowship along with studying the Word in Bible Study Fellowship. I became a believer. As C. S. Lewis said, "Believing in Christianity is like believing in the rising sun, it's not simply that you can see it, but by it you can see everything else." God revealed Himself to me through my belief of the claims of Jesus Christ. I once was blind, but now I see. So what is the answer? I believe the great spiritual paradox is at play here: victory is won through surrender!

Step 12 clearly stated that the purpose of these steps is to have a "Spiritual Awakening" as the result of working the steps. The Bible claims that we are all spiritually dead and therefore subject to God's wrath. The problem is that spiritually dead people cannot receive the gift of the gospel. Apostle Paul says in 1 Corinthians 2:14, "The man without the Spirit does not accept the things that come from the Spirit of God, for they are foolishness to him, and he cannot understand them, because they are spiritually discerned."

In other words, we are blinded by the ways of the world. As apostle Paul said, "The god of this age has blinded the minds of unbelievers, so that they cannot see the light of the gospel that displays the glory of Christ, who is the image of God" (2 Corinthians 11:14). The Bible claims that we are spirituality blind and unable to recognize our need for God's help or if you will a Savior. We are held in bondage to our sinful nature and we live in a world that is hostile to God. The Bible paints a dreadful picture of our condition but the Bible also gives us our only hope by God's great love and mercy making us alive in Christ. "But because of his great love for us, God, who is rich in mercy, made us alive with Christ even when we were dead in transgressions—it is by grace you have been saved . . . For it is grace you have been saved, through faith—and this is not from yourselves, it is the gift of God—not by works, so that no one can boast" (Ephesians 2:4–9).

The Big Book makes similar claims by painting the same dire picture in step 1—stating that we are powerless over alcohol (depravity) and our life is unmanageable. This presents us with what seems as a hopeless state of mind. But like the Bible, the Twelve-Step Program provides a solution that could only be obtained by experiencing a Spiritual Awakening and finding a loving merciful God. The Big Book also claims that we need to be in a desperate state in order to humble ourselves enough to accept help of any kind. As I stated in "My Story," the hardest thing I had ever done was to cry out those few simple words: "I can't do it . . . I need help." Pride had taken me to the bitter end and it was only by the gift of desperation that I was able humble myself and ask for help. The Big Book describes this beautifully . . . "We, in turn, sought the same escape with all the desperation of drowning men. What seemed at first a flimsy reed has proved to be the loving and powerful hand of God."

Both the Bible and the Big Book maintain that we must have a spiritual awakening in order to see the light of the truth. This is not an intellectual exercise. In fact, the intellect is all too often a hindrance to overcoming our spiritual blindness. It is the intellect that makes the case that we are not that bad through the use of rationalization and self-justification. Again, it is our pride and our sinful nature that keeps us in the shadows and living the big lie—"I'm not that bad." So what is the solution? God is the answer. God makes us spiritually alive. And it is only then that we can begin to see the truth. The truth is that we must quit the argument and make a decision (third step) to trust God.

But the reason we make that decision is because God has made us spiritually alive. It is all God's doing. All we have to do is make a decision. We have come to a fork in the road and the choice is simple: continue on the path of the self-centered life or take the path leading to a God-centered life. It's a no-brainer; it's a choice of life or death. We can keep on fighting to the bitter end or we can surrender to the process and be given a new life. What is your choice to be?

The title of this book is "God Won" . . . "It is finished!" This phrase is in the past tense. The plan of salvation has been put in place by the Father, and was purchased by Jesus Christ on the cross, and is applied in our daily life by the Holy Spirit. It all seems so inconceivable that the plan of salvation which was put in place at the foundation of the world is based on us having to surrender in order to win. But the fact of my life is that my nature has been fighting God all along. Genesis explains this with the Fall of Adam . . . choosing to live for ourselves rather than the glory of God. The Big Book says that we had to "quit playing God . . . And we have ceased fighting anything or anyone." The Bible makes it clear that, "It is done." In other words, there are no conditions; no fight or struggle remains. The fight is over and God won! Three different times in Scripture God proclaims that His work is completed:

(a) In Genesis, God says it is *good.*
(b) In the Gospel, Jesus says it is *finished.*

(c) In Revelation, Jesus says, it is *done*.

God has left nothing unfinished. God says, "It is done. I am the Alpha and the Omega, the Beginning and the End. To the thirsty, I will give water without cost from the spring of the water of life. Those who are victorious will inherit all this, and I will be their God and they will be my children. But the cowardly, the unbelieving . . . they will be consigned to the fiery lake of burning sulfur. This is the second death" (Revelation 21:6–8). God goes further to explain that for those who are conquerors will never be separated from God. As we shared early on in this book, once God strikes and invades our heart and soul He never let's go. One of the most revered passages of the Bible, speaks about nothing in all creation can separate us from the love of God. In fact, Romans 8:35–39 Paul says, "In all these things we are more than conquerors through him who loved us. For I am convinced that neither death nor life, neither angels nor demons, neither the present nor the future, nor any powers, neither height nor depth, nor anything else in all creation, will be able to separate us from the love of God that is in Christ Jesus our Lord."

The road to victory is narrow, but the path to the gates of hell is broad. Few of us find the way to victory. Only a small fraction of alcoholics in recovery stay sober beyond ninety days and even a fraction of those make it beyond a year. God only knows the percent of those sitting in the church pews that have been truly converted, but surely the percent is but a small fraction. The story of the lepers in the Bible is similar to the story of the alcoholic in the Big Book and their position is much the same as yours. We all have a spiritual malady and if you remain where you are, you will perish; if you go to Jesus you will live.

The endless question is why do some get it and others don't. By all outward appearances, we surrender but the life-saving results of God's grace do not materialize for many. Some are blessed, but many are not. As Jesus said on the Sermon in the Mount, "Blessed are the poor in spirit, for theirs is the kingdom of heaven. Blessed are those who mourn…Blessed are the meek, for they will inherit the earth" (Matthew 5: 3-5). In other words, we cannot experience God-blessed salvation without true humility. Again, it is pride that stands in the way of our dealing with our destructive sinful ways. We may believe that we have surrendered, but in truth, we continue to rebel against God. It is only when we mourn and grieve over our persecution of God and truly humble ourselves at the foot of the cross, that we will receive God's comfort and blessings. "For just as we share abundantly in the suffering of Christ, so also our comfort abounds through Christ" (2 Corinthians 1: 5)'.

God spoke through Moses in Deuteronomy 30:15–20, "Now listen! Today I am giving you a choice between life and death; between prosperity and disaster . . . You can make this choice by loving the Lord your God, obeying Him, and committing yourself firmly to Him. *This is the key to your life.*" The choice is simple. Continue on the broad road of this self-centered life and die or choose the narrow God-centered path and receive the gift of the eternal life by the grace of God. It is a simple choice, but not easy. In fact, it is the most difficult and the most important decision one can make. It is a matter of life or death. The disciple Thomas was a skeptic like so many of us. Thomas was devoted and loyal to Jesus but even he refused to examine the evidence and was deluded into bitter unbelief, yet Jesus loved him still and had come to him. Jesus literally said to Thomas, "stop doubting and believe" (John 20:27). Jesus commanded Thomas to make his life choice. Would it be deadly unbelief or a life of obedient faith?

We discussed early on, it is a matter of herculean courage for one to make the decision of ultimate surrender. The thing that we need is the last thing that we want. What we need is God's help, which is the last thing we want. In fact, we fight God and relay on ourselves. To completely give up our right to ourselves is next to impossible for the self-willed, self-centered sinners that we all are. We often ask why God doesn't just save us. Why must we surrender our will?

Why doesn't God do everything we ask? After all, He is sovereign and in complete control. This is exactly the point. God has done His part by Jesus Christ paying the price and shedding His blood on the cross and fulfilling the Fathers plan of salvation. God has finished His part. He has left the heavenly throne and come down to earth to dwell among us and pay the ultimate price for our salvation. Now we must do our part.

God accomplished the greatest event in human history. God gave us His love through His Son on the Cross. The Cross didn't just happen. The Cross is the center of God's plan from the foundation of the world. The Cross of Christ is God's revelation of the truth regarding His judgment of sin. Justice requires judgment. A price has to be paid. And God paid that price through His Son on the Cross. The Cross of Christ is the gate by which all humankind can enter into oneness with God. Jesus Christ made it possible for the entire human race to come home to a right relationship with God. The purpose of Christ coming was to die for our sins on the Cross. He is "the Lamb who was slain from the foundation of the world" (Revelation 13:8). God came in the flesh to take away our sins and nothing else. The Cross is where the holiness of God collides with the sinfulness of man. This tremendous collision is the greatest event in all eternity where the way to the new life is found. But it is not sinful man that bears the cost and pain of this collision. It is God's love that pays the price.

The only question that remains is—will I take the ultimate step to enter into a right relationship with Him? All the great blessings of God are finished and complete, but they are not mine until I enter into a relationship with Him on His terms. This is not an intellectual act, but a deliberate act of my will to commit myself. But will I commit, abiding myself completely and absolutely in God. We must do this or it will kill us. There must be a surrender of the will and not surrender to some persuasive or compelling argument. The greatest moment of our life is upon us. We must quit the argument and exercise our will and place our complete faith and trust in Him. So how do we do this? Where do we get the courage? The answer is that God makes it possible. The great spiritual paradox is that victory is won by surrender.

Once we decide that sin must die in us and not simply be restrained, contained or suppressed, but be crucified with Christ on the Cross who died to sin of the world.

Again, we must make this decision of a lifetime on our own. The only way is to find time alone with Christ and to our innermost self make the moral decision that sin in your life must be put to death. Speak directly to Jesus Christ and explain that you identify with His death on the Cross and decide that sin in you must be put to death. As Paul said in Romans 6: 6, "Our old man was crucified with Him, that the body of sin might be done away with, that we should no longer be slaves of sin." Once we have been crucified with Christ, all that remains in our flesh is the newborn life of Christ. "I have been crucified with Christ and I no longer live, but Christ lives in me." (Galatians 2: 20).

The game of life is rigged and God won! The Father has planned for our salvation. The Son has purchased our salvation on the cross and the Holy Spirit applies our salvation to our daily lives. Our part in this plan is to place our faith and trust in God through an absolute surrender. I cannot explain how this works. I do not have an explanation, but in my case, I do have a formulation in the promises of the Twelve-Step Recovery Program of Alcoholics Anonymous leading to a spiritual awakening which revealed to me the Good News of the Gospel of Jesus Christ. The new life is born. Glory is to God!

ABOUT THE AUTHOR

⎯⎯⎯⎯⎯⎯ ❧⤳☙ ⎯⎯⎯⎯⎯⎯

Donald C. Wes was born and raised in Southern California and educated at the University of Southern California in business and finance and received his master's degree in finance from California State University. He had an accomplished career in the healthcare industry as a developer and executive officer. Donald is married with three children and six grandchildren. Currently, he and his wife are semi-retired while owning and operating a nationwide real estate company. Today, Donald has fifteen years of sobriety and is an active member of the AA fellowship as well as an active participant in Bible Study Fellowship.

CPSIA information can be obtained
at www.ICGtesting.com
Printed in the USA
BVHW070956070119
537204BV00010B/318/P